THE
MARTINI
COCKTAIL

A Meditation on the World's Greatest Drink,
with Recipes

ROBERT SIMONSON

Photographs by Lizzie Munro

TEN SPEED PRESS
California | New York

To Robert Odin Simonson Sr., Martini drinker (1928–2019).

Contents

Prologue:
My Dad's Martini
1

Introduction:
Bewildering Depths
5

The Story
9

The Recipes
69

Epilogue:
My Martini
154

Appendix 1:
Martini Accoutrements
157

Appendix 2:
Martini Quotes
159

Acknowledgments
161

Index
162

Lines in Dispraise of Dispraise

I hereby bequeath to the bid-a-wee home all people who
have statistics to prove that a human

Is nothing but a combination of iron and water and
potash and albumen.

That may very well be the truth

But it's just like saying that a cocktail in nothing but ice
and gin and vermouth.

—Ogden Nash

Prologue
My Dad's Martini

I grew up in an average American household. When cocktail hour came along, my mother had an Old-Fashioned and my father had a Martini—the apple pie and rare steak of American drinking. Neither wavered in their preference over the years. As was the case with many of their generation, they had their drinks and they stuck to them. Unlike other men of his era, my father wasn't overly fussy about his Martini. He didn't have a favorite gin—whatever was cheapest would do, usually Mr. Boston—and he drank his Martinis on the rocks, holding the glass in the same hand as one of his Kent cigarettes.

But, like any Martini drinker, he insisted on a few particulars. He thought the whole dry Martini–vermouth atomizer ethos ridiculous, and always included a fair measure of vermouth in his drinks. Believe it or not, he liked the flavor of vermouth. He also slipped in a little olive brine; not too much, just a quarter of a teaspoon to, in his words, "enhance the taste of the olive." And he was respectful of the drink's potency.

"Unless you sip it, you're going to drink too much," he told me. "It's too strong. On the rocks, it's diluted, so you don't have to worry about how fast you're drinking it. Younger people, when they're starting to drink, tend to serve too many. They down them like Coke. And they're very aggressive at refilling. You could get loaded pretty quickly.

"A lot of our drinking was done at house parties, dinners," he continued. "We had this group who would take turns serving dinner. Same group, every month. There were always cocktails first, ad infinitum."

When I asked why he drank Martinis, he shrugged and said, "It was just something I did every day at five o'clock." But why not another cocktail? What is it about the Martini?

He paused, struggling for the right words. "It has a unique flavor," he began. "You really get a shock out of it, especially the first sip. It doesn't knock you out, but it's a definite shock, the feeling and the taste. It makes you sit up and pay attention." He paused again. "I keep coming back to the word 'shock.'"

He agreed with me that it was important that the drink be very cold. "But," he added, "I never had a problem with that. They didn't last too long."

Introduction
Bewildering Depths

As a young man, back in 1991, with little thought of
devoting my time to writing prose poems to mixed drinks, I
was—completely without justification, mind you—instinctually
fussy about Martinis. One night, while enjoying a good meal at
an elegant country inn in Vermont, I ordered a gin Martini and
then waited, impatiently, as the completed cocktail sat on the
service bar getting warmer and warmer by the second. When the
youthful waiter finally brought the drink to my table, beads of
condensation were streaming down the glass. The cocktail had an
unappetizing, lukewarm look to it. It made me shudder. Muster-
ing up a starchy hauteur I didn't know I possessed, I turned to the
poor waiter and said, "Excuse me, but I think this is undrinkable."
He took it back, like a corked bottle of wine.

I don't blame my youth for my imperious behavior. I blame
the Martini. The drink's outsize reputation does things to a
human's mind.

Gin, vermouth, sometimes bitters, lemon twist or olive, and
lots of opinions. Those are the ingredients of a Martini. But the
last item is the most important. It's the one that keeps us talking

about a drink that is nearly 150 years old. Something about the Martini gets people worked up, certain that the world might have a fighting chance at decency if only people would adhere to their particular recipe.

I'm pretty certain that you out there, reading this sentence, think you know a little something about what makes a good Martini, even if you've never had one. But, let me tell you, everything you know about the Martini is wrong.

Think you know who invented the world's most famous cocktail? You're wrong. Think you know where and when it was created? Wrong again. Insist that it must be made with gin? Nope. Vodka? Uh-uh. Positive it should be stirred; should be shaken; properly takes a lemon twist as garnish; actually asks for an olive; requires a portion of dry vermouth in order to bear the name; should be kept well away from vermouth at all costs; calls for orange bitters; doesn't need orange bitters; can be served on the rocks; should only be served up; should be presented in a Martini glass; demands a coupe? Wrong. All wrong.

Or, *right*, actually. The thing is, when it comes to the Martini, everyone thinks they've got the straight dope. But the certain don't always agree—sometimes don't ever agree. So some of these know-it-alls must be wrong. But which ones? Thus, everyone is wrong about the Martini, because everyone is right about the Martini, and *everyone* can't be right. Get it?

No? Well, I don't blame you. It's a confusing subject, but also a rich one. So rich that whole books have been devoted to the drink. The volume you hold in your hands is hardly the first. In 1981, Lowell Edmunds, a classics professor at Rutgers University, gave the cocktail the thesis treatment in his book *The Silver Bullet: The Martini in American Civilization*. Nobody blinked; nobody thought he was crazy. Of course, a man with a doctorate would take the Martini seriously. Of course he would. One decade, the 1990s, produced a veritable boom in Martini books, all hoping to cash in on the Martini revival then underway.

The drink seems to have held an unyielding grip on the American imagination from the very first. Recipes only began to appear in cocktail manuals in the 1880s. But, by then, it was already an object of fascination. On July 30, 1887, the Long Island Wheelmen (that is, bicyclists) gathered on Fulton Street, in downtown Brooklyn, for one of their monthly smokers. There was entertainment, and before it began, a Captain Charles Luscomb assumed the podium. "Search," he declared, "if you will, the blazing coruscations of Tiffany's; wander amazed through the art galleries of the metropolis; aye, even sample the bewildering depths of the 'Martini cocktail,' and you will find nothing that can compare with, meet, or equal the elegant tribute that is now about to be bestowed upon you."

Just a few years old, and the Martini was already the equal of Tiffany's jewels. Not a bad start.

The planet has never ceased plumbing those bewildering depths. Sometimes that only means getting to the bottom of the glass, and then another and another. Many other times, though, the dive is about getting to the bottom of the drink conceptually, philosophically. Why do we like the Martini so much? Why do we drink them so often? Why do we fight over it as if it were some vague-ish amendment to the Constitution, the interpretation of which the Founding Fathers left to future generations to work out?

I don't promise to answer these questions any better than previous generations. (After all, previous generations weren't very good at it, either, or we wouldn't still be arguing about the matter.) But I promise to give the Martini a good going over. And there will be opinions. Lots of opinions.

The Story

The "Latecomer"

The King of Cocktails was late to the cocktail party. American drinkers had lived under many other liquid monarchs—the Mint Julep, Sherry Cobbler, and Whiskey Cocktail—before they even heard the word "Martini." The difference with the Martini is, once it climbed upon that throne, it never stepped down, nor was it usurped or overthrown. The king was here to stay.

The Martini wasn't even the first of its breed, or the most famous. That new and exciting mixer, vermouth, was paired first with whiskey and won quick fame in the Manhattan. The first mention of the Manhattan in a cocktail book came in 1884. The Martini made its cocktail-book bow four years later, in 1888, in both Harry Johnson's updated edition of his *Bartender's Manual* and Theodore Proulx's Chicago-printed *Bartender's Manual*. (The volume by Proulx, a French-Canadian who later prospered as a lawyer, also marked the debut of the Old-Fashioned in a book.) Proulx described the Martini as "half Tom gin and half vermouth made like any other cocktail; no absinthe." "Tom" refers to Old Tom gin, a then-prevalent, sweeter form of gin. The type of vermouth is not specified, but was likely sweet vermouth from Italy; dry vermouth did not find a home in the Martini cocktail until later.

Proulx's Martini, then, was a decidedly sweetish drink, as were all Martinis in the beginning. The recipe in Harry Johnson's *Bartender's Manual* added dashes of bitters, curaçao, and gum syrup (a sugar syrup made with gum Arabic), making the drink even sweeter. This made Johnson's Martini not terribly different from the Martinez, a cocktail that first appeared in a book in 1884, and is included in an 1887 reprinting of the *Bar-Tender's Guide* by the father of mixology, Jerry Thomas (who was by that time deceased). The main difference was that Thomas's Martinez asked for dashes of maraschino liqueur. Because of the similarities, and the relative sameness of their names, the Martinez is commonly, if not conclusively, believed to be an immediate predecessor to the Martini. (More on that later.)

Once the Martini hit the scene, it and the Manhattan were rarely apart—on menus, in news stories, or in cocktail books. But they were more frenemies than friends, forever vying for cocktail supremacy. The Manhattan had the initial edge, but it didn't keep it for long.

By 1893, the *St. Louis Post-Dispatch*, weighing in on the matter, said, "The Manhattan cocktail was once almost the national drink. It is still the standard in the cocktail line, but the Martini, which has been growing in favor from year to year, is now almost as much called for in this city as the Manhattan. Both of these drinks are said to be good appetizers, but there are men who drink as many after meals as before. The Manhattan cocktail, as is fairly well known, is a mixture of whiskey and vermouth. The base of the Martini cocktail is gin." This article was reprinted extensively in other papers, so there was little chance that Sunny Jim of Seattle or Good-Time Charlie of Chattanooga missed the intelligence. The Martini was the "it" drink.

In 1901, the press was still rubbing in the Manhattan's new also-ran status, while already promulgating the never-to-die myth that Martinis are hard to make well. "Martini cocktails are very difficult to produce perfectly," wrote the *New York Sun*, adding that the drink "to a great extent has entirely replaced the old Whiskey Cocktail and Manhattan."

Ouch. One can just hear the old sad-sack Manhattan crying out from his stool at the end of the bar, "But, *I was here first.*"

Portrait of Vermouth as a Young Wine

To understand why the Martini and Manhattan were so closely associated with one another, and, indeed, sometimes confused with one another in the early years, one has to look at the nature of vermouth in the nineteenth century, particularly its color.

We are accustomed to an image of the Manhattan as a drink with a deep amber color, while the Martini is crystal clear. At the time of their first flush of fame, however, they might have been mistaken for twins. The whiskeys used in Manhattans may not have been aged for long, and, thus, didn't have the darker hue we are accustomed to,

which comes from aging in wood barrels. At the same time, sweet vermouth was much lighter in color than it is today, and dry vermouth was much darker; the addition of caramel to sweet vermouth to distinguish it from dry was not yet a common practice. Hence, the usual description of vermouths in cocktail books of the time was "Italian" and "French"; "red" and "white" would have made no sense to bartenders and drinkers back then.

According to author and vermouth expert François Monti, as late as 1914, Italian vermouth was still described in the United States as having a "deep golden color." The French vermouths reaching the United States were also on the amber side, and likely, when mixed with gin in roughly equal amounts, produced a cocktail that would look today like a rather watery Manhattan. The two drinks were not the only cocktails visually confused with one another. In 1899, the *New York Sun* even observed about the Rob Roy, the Manhattan's Scotch-based cousin, "When completed . . . looked not unlike a Martini cocktail."

The Martini's reputation as a tinted cocktail would continue for decades. In 1891, the *St. Louis Republic*, surveying the current drink scene, noted "the dainty pale-gold tint" of the then-ascendant Martini. In "The Short Cut," a bit of light verse from 1909 about three sodden poseurs named Punk, Bogg, and Slush, the poet talks of how the three "cuddled the amber Martini and mixed with the friendly high-ball."

One year earlier, in an interview in the *Evening World* newspaper with Mary MacLane, the so-called Wild Woman of Butte, the bisexual memoirist muses about British music-hall star Alice Lloyd. "I am fascinated right now by Alice Lloyd," said MacLane. "I can't explain to you the fascination she has for me. . . . I would like to see her drink a Martini cocktail, because a Martini with its amber light would suit her."

In the 1926 novel *Dry Martini* by John Thomas, the protagonist receives a Martini that is a "fragrant amber." As late as the 1930s, poet Ogden Nash memorably rhymed about "a yellow, a mellow Martini."

All these references to hue look downright bizarre to a world that has long known only the see-through Martini. Slowly but surely,

European producers filtered the color out of dry vermouth. Put that together with Americans' habit of putting less and less vermouth in a Martini as the twentieth century marched on, and you get a drink that had less and less color, until it has none at all. Voilà! The mid-twentieth-century Martini in all its invisible nothingness.

A Clubman's Drink

Socially speaking, the Martini is a paradox. Though enjoyed by millions, it retains a reputation as an elite cocktail: a sophisticated, stylish, and cultured thing that is enjoyed by people who can be described the same way. The drink didn't stumble into this rep. It seems to have worn it from the very first.

"Clubman" isn't a descriptor you hear very often anymore. But once upon a time in America, the term conjured up a sort of character recognizable to every citizen: privileged, upper crust, soft, sporty, dandyish, somewhat decadent. A clubman belonged to posh clubs, the sort where, to attain membership, you had to travel in the right circles or come from the right family. Most of these clubs had bars inside and, from the 1880s on, those bars apparently served a lot of Martinis.

Americans liked to gawk at the wealthy then as they do now, so club life was a source of regular fodder for newspapers. And when reports of Martinis made the dailies, it was often in connection with the drinking preferences of clubs and clubmen.

As early as 1893, the *Atlanta Constitution* declared that "the fastidious clubman . . . is particular about the right amount of vermouth in his Martini cocktail." In a 1902 article titled "With the Clubman," the *New York Times* wrote, "At the Calumet a favorite drink before dinner is the Hall cocktail, named in honor of Frank de Peyster Hall, for a long time one of the Governors of the club. It is a great improvement on the popular Martini and has a dash of absinthe as one of the ingredients."

Two years later, the subject of a Martini filched at a club was news enough to merit a few inches in the *New York Times*. Apparently, a clubman was charged for two Martinis, but received only one, the other having been drunk in transit by a crafty bellboy. Another article that year went so far as to say the Martini was so clubbable that it was invented at a club, the Manhattan Club (which is commonly believed to be the birthplace of the Manhattan cocktail).

The Martini's highbrow associations stuck in the American mind. In 1909, the *Emporia Gazette* observed, "The multi-millionaire, in popular imagination, is given to Sybaritic tastes that run the gamut from domestic infidelity to an insane appetite for Martini cocktails and champagne." The same year, the *Santa Cruz Evening News* stated, "We believe the working man going home from his labors is as much entitled to his glass of beer as the millionaire is to his Martini cocktail in his club." Six decades later, the *Esquire Drink Book* described the Yale, Harvard, and Princeton Clubs "and similar places where college men forgather" as "hotbeds of bias," where Martini recipes were concerned.

It is perhaps no accident then, that way back in 1892 when the Heublein company of Connecticut decided to sell bottled cocktails, including the Martini, they christened the line "Club Cocktails."

Mr. Popularity

The Martini's rise was meteoric. It was a mere decade or so old when it first emerged as a drink with few peers. Gin distillers advertised their product's aptness for making Martinis. A variety of bottled cocktail brands hit the market, and the Martini was always among the proffered mixes. By the mid-1890s, the Martini was routinely mentioned nationwide in advertisements for restaurants and saloons, typically in conjunction with the Manhattan. The most fabulous society meals of the day, held in hotels and halls, had their menus reprinted in the newspapers the next day, and the bill of fare almost always began with a Martini.

"The drink most affected by men about town at present, whenever they feel in need of a gentle stimulant and a not too potent appetizer," reported the *St. Louis Republic* in 1891, "is the Martini cocktail." The *Brooklyn Eagle*, that same year, told of an American who walked into an English barroom and became indignant when the barmaid did not know how to make a Martini cocktail. Women in America, however, did know. "Wives who entertain their husband's friends now," wrote the *New York's Morning Telegraph*, also in 1891, "take a pride in being able to concoct a Manhattan, a Vermouth, or a Martini cocktail."

Old-timers were occasionally puzzled by all the Martini madness. One man, quoted in the *Detroit Free Press* in 1898, noted the cocktail wasn't much different from another that had been enjoyed years before. "As the Turf Club cocktail [page 92]," he said, "it was popular nearly twenty years ago, and the only change there has been in it since that time is in the name. Yet only a few years ago the Martini cocktail was looked upon as something new."

By 1909, the drink was so entrenched in American society that, when the *Philadelphia Enquirer* noted the death of Tom Fay, bartender at the ritzy Rittenhouse Club, they took care to mention that Fay was known for his skill in making a Martini.

Martini, Who Are You Anyway?

But what was this Martini that so bewitched the clubmen and the newspaper reporters who covered them? No one was altogether sure. It had gin in it, and vermouth. That seemed certain. But what kind? And how much of each? And was there anything else needed? Harry Johnson's recipe (see page 82) and Theodore Proulx's recipe (see page 83) differ enough from one another to be different cocktails. Bartender George J. Kappeler's recipe, introduced in 1895, was similar to Johnson's with the addition of a lemon twist and "cherry if desired." In *How to Mix Fancy Drinks* (1903), orange bitters and Peychaud's bitters came into play. The drink's trimmings were all over the map.

Publishers and bartenders appeared to have sensed this confusion over one of the nation's most popular drinks because, around the turn of the twentieth century, books began running recipes titled "Martini No. 1," "Martini No. 2," and so on, each one a little different from the next. This trend reached its apotheosis in the 1930s with the publication of *Swallows* (1930), a reprint of San Francisco barman Bill Boothby's 1908 book, but with different recipes; and *Here's How* by George A. Lurie (1933). Both volumes contained no fewer than *nine* different Martini recipes.

The differences between the recipes were stark. In *Swallows*, the basic Martini was composed of equal parts gin and Italian vermouth, two dashes bitters, a pickled onion, and a lemon twist. The "Martini No. 2" was made of two-thirds gin, one-third Italian vermouth, two dashes orange bitters, two dashes Angostura bitters, a pickled onion, and a lemon twist. The "Martini No. 3" retreated into simplicity, asking for only two-thirds gin, one-third Italian vermouth, and two dashes orange bitters.

French vermouth finally comes into play in *Swallows'* four different "Martini Dry" recipes. And in those, we finally see a few olives.

The matter of garnish was a Martini minefield all its own. Since, in the drink's early years, there was a lot of overlap among the various recipes in terms of dryness and sweetness, there was no set dogma yet as to what the cocktail's proper garnish should be. But the decision seemed to be based generally on what sort of Martini you were talking about. Whenever dry vermouth was involved, olives and twists were usually called for; onions were also occasionally dropped in (long before that garnish became exclusively linked to the Gibson). When dealing with a sweet Martini (a common recipe back then), which used sweet vermouth, the garnish was often a cherry. The Martini cherry—so odd a suggestion to us today—was not a wild aberration then, but a common sight. As late as 1917, the *Morning Tulsa Daily World*, reporting on a speech by one F. J. Kemb, of Columbia University, wrote, "He spoke of Tulsa's streets as 'smooth as the cheek of the cherry in a Martini cocktail,' a simile that scored big."

Often, however, there appeared to be little rhyme or reason to garnish selection. Some recipes in cocktail books paired the lemon peel and olive (a move still seen today); others teamed the lemon peel and cherry. Still others suggested garnishes be added only "if desired." A couple of recipes from the turn of the last century actually instructed "cherry or olive," as if they were interchangeable. (Manhattans suffered similar garnish confusion at the time.)

A reporter at the *Allentown Leader* saw sufficient reader interest in this issue to devote a half column to the subject on June 21, 1899. His contention, based on bartender intelligence, was that the Martini cherry was on its way out, and the olive on its way in. He theorized:

> It is a fad containing a grain of common sense, which is as follows. An ordinary Martini cocktail is composed of gin, vermouth, bitters, and syrup. It has a bitter-sweet flavor. A brandied cherry is customarily served with it, as also with the Manhattan. . . . Many drinkers object to the cherry, however, because it leaves so sweet a taste in the mouth. Others prefer to omit the syrup, too, in which case the cocktail is called "dry," in imitation of the phase [sic] "dry" champagne, which is champagne without much sugar in it. Now, the addition of cherry to a dry cocktail is ridiculous, because it imparts to the concoction that very sweetness that the drinker wishes to avoid. . . . Hence some ingenious mixer of drinks has cast about for a substitute for the brandied cherry, and has hit on the stoneless olive. It is a happy idea because it provides a fitting tidbit for the dry cocktails.

Sound logic, and well expressed. *Or*, perhaps just a sales pitch from your friendly local olive salesman, as the article ends with instructions about where you can purchase these trendy cocktail olives.

The Sweet Martini: A Defense

One of the common ways in which cocktail books from the 1900s through the 1930s divided Martini recipes was into "dry," "medium," and "sweet" versions. This seems perverse by the standards of the last seventy-five years, in which people have been thinking of Martinis as either "dry" or "very dry." But, in considering the history of

the drink, one must never forget that the Martini started out as a sweet drink, made with two sweet things—Old Tom gin and sweet vermouth, and some other sugary items as well, like gum syrup, curaçao, and maraschino liqueur. The drink's march to dryness began almost immediately—first by the substitution of dry vermouth for the sweet, then by the replacement of Old Tom with London dry gin, and finally by the slow, steady elimination of vermouth altogether. But that journey took decades, and, during that slow transition, there were still plenty of sane people walking around who preferred the sweet rendition. It was the original, after all. The dry Martini was the parvenu.

Sweet Martini recipes usually called for sweet vermouth. The medium Martini was basically a "perfect" Martini, calling for an equal split between sweet and dry vermouth. Starting in the 1940s, these variations began to disappear, to be replaced instead by recipes for "Martini," "Martini Dry," and "Martini Very Dry." This last, in the *Cocktail and Wine Digest*, which was published annually by bartender Oscar Haimo of New York's The Pierre hotel, called for 2¾ ounces of gin and a mere 2 dashes of dry vermouth.

The sweet Martini is barely remembered today. When it is, it's regarded as an abomination. The reaction is understandable. The drink is nothing like what we know now as a Martini. But, prepared well, it is by no means a bad drink, and one that ought to be honored, if only because it is the ancestor of the cocktail we know and love so dearly.

For this reason, I've included a Sweet Martini in the recipe section of this book (page 86). Give it a try. The name need not be an oxymoron.

Lies, Lies, and More Lies

"Never let the truth get in the way of a good story."

That epigram came from the mind of Mark Twain. But it is a favorite of Dale DeGroff, celebrated bartender and one of the founders of the cocktail renaissance we are all currently lapping up. I've heard him say it on several occasions. And, while it always tugs a smile from my lips, the idea behind it gives me pause.

DeGroff has reason to like a good story. Tall tales are part of the arsenal of every good bartender, along with a ready smile, a joke or two, and a bit of insight into the local sports scene. If the cocktail a customer has ordered has a fun backstory, however specious, that customer is going to be all the happier for having ordered it. It's a twofer: intoxication with a side of infotainment. Nobody wants to be slapped in the face with the facts when they're in a bar. They came to the bar to *escape* facts.

This is perhaps why, despite recent efforts by a small army of folks like me to dispel the thick fog bank surrounding cocktail history, the same old fables and legends stubbornly persist. More cling to the Martini than any other cocktail. This is understandable. An unclaimed winning lottery ticket is going to root out plenty of sticky-fingered claimants.

But none of these stories is *the* story. Not even close. The two central facts about the Martini are: it's the most famous cocktail in history, and we don't know where it came from. That's a hard reality to swallow. So, just as humans do with the whole meaning-of-life question, we keep chasing after the truth, trotting out the same familiar yarns year after year, hoping it'll all come together and make sense one day.

I've been aware of the prevailing Martini origin myths for years. But, in my research for this book, I encountered several more I hadn't before. One 1904 account said the drink was first compounded by one Judge Martine at the Manhattan Club in New York. At a 1932 trial to decide if the Martini & Rossi vermouth outfit owned rights to the name Martini, one witness said the drink "was invented by an Irish bartender in the St. Charles Hotel at New Orleans and was originally called a St. Martine cocktail." Rival vermouth maker Cinzano, however, claimed the drink was invented by a "New Orleans bartender named Martinez." A member of the Rossi family, Count Ernesto Rossi di Montelera, went further afield, saying in 1930 that the drink was invented in Torino.

In 1902, a whimsical bit of nonsense by one "Poeta Pants" appeared in the *Chicago Tribune*. It told of a Martini-drinking Mr. Criticus Flubb-Dubbe, who insisted "it was named by a musician in memory of Padre Martini, the celebrated composer and historian of the Bolognese school. The form of this cocktail is correct, and contrapuntally it is extremely interesting. Above all, it has the same seductive quality as the illustrious Bolognese. I am very fond of polyphonic drinks." So, you see, people were waxing ludicrous on the origins of the Martini early on.

But when the Martini meets a news cycle, as it periodically does, it is three central tales that are dependably repeated. Let's start with the most disposable and disprovable: The Knickerbocker Hotel, the Beaux Arts lodging that, upon opening in 1906, was immediately the most swank place to stay in the then on-the-cusp Times Square, had a bartender named Martini di Arma di Taggia. John D. Rockefeller walked in and asked for a new drink, and the barkeep handed him a mix of gin, dry vermouth, and orange bitters. The titan liked it and called it the Martini.

One could blow up any number of details of this fairy tale (Rockefeller was a teetotaler, for one), but the date gives the whole game away. The Martini had walked the earth for twenty-odd years by the time the Knickerbocker opened. However, this hasn't stopped the Knickerbocker, now a luxury residence, from promoting itself as a probable home of the drink. It's complete bunk.

The town of Martinez, California, has gone the Knickerbocker one better. They put up a plaque declaring their Bay Area community to be the birthplace of the Martini. (And everyone knows that plaques don't lie.) The Martinez story goes like this: It's 1849. The Gold Rush is on. In a scene straight out of some hoary 1930s film, a miner walks into the town saloon. He has struck it rich and wants to celebrate the way most miners do, by tying one on. The bartender, Julio Richelieu, decides to offer him something original called the Martinez Special. The miner approves. As soon as he gets to San Francisco, he asks for a Martinez Special, explaining what the drink is to the confused barmen. Word spread of the wondrous cocktail. A legend was born.

San Francisco, not content to accept the sloppy seconds of little old Martinez, has its own version of the Martini's debut, making for the third most-common tale. This one involves the great nineteenth-century mixologist Jerry Thomas. Again, a pesky traveler stumbles in complaining of thirst. And, again, the bartender, for untold reasons, decides to serve him something completely new. (These nineteenth-century California bartenders sure liked to make extra work for themselves.) Again, the bartender decides to name it after Martinez, because that was the traveler's next stop. (Take note that both of the Bay Area myths only carry weight if you already believe that the Martinez is the father of the Martini.)

The boring, but most likely story of the birth of the Martini is that a cocktail made of gin and vermouth probably evolved naturally in multiple bars in multiple locations around the same time, once those premises came into possession of vermouth and a barman with a modicum of imagination.

The Name

The source of the Martini's very name is as debated as the origin of the cocktail. As mentioned previously, some think it a liquid and linguistic evolution of "Martinez." Some claim a connection to the Martini-Henry rifle, used by the British army beginning in 1871. Both gun and cocktail, it was frequently joked, possess a good deal of firepower. And Martini & Rossi, the Italian vermouth brand, has long contended that it gave the famous cocktail its name. As soon as the early 1900s, in a series of advertisements, the company declared, "The real Martini cocktail must be made with Martini & Rossi Italian Vermouth" and "Martini & Rossi Italian Vermouth is the foundation of the Original and only Genuine Martini Cocktail."

Such boasting aside, there's a lot of common sense to the vermouth company's claim. Martini Sola & Co., as the firm was then called, first shipped one hundred cases of their sweet *rosso* vermouth to the United States in 1867, according to company documents and Anna Scudellari, the archivist and historian for Martini & Rossi. (Again, remember the Martini was first made with sweet vermouth.) Advertisements for the vermouth began to appear several years later, and the company further promoted their product by entering it in competitions, such as the

1876 Centennial International Exhibition in Philadelphia. Martini &
Rossi was the leading vermouth in the US market.

It doesn't take much of a leap of logic to imagine a bartender or
a patron referring to a gin cocktail made with vermouth as a Martini
cocktail. (Think of the Dubonnet cocktail, which is just gin with
Dubonnet added.) It's the Occam's razor answer to the name question.
Scholars and journalists tend to dismiss the Martini & Rossi theory out
of hand because it smacks of corporate PR. And they are right to be
suspicious. Liquor companies have always been self-serving fable fab-
ricators. They lie more than they tell the truth. But this seems a special
case, as it has logic on its side. To have on one hand a famous cocktail
called the Martini, which requires vermouth, and on the other hand a
prominent vermouth company called Martini, and to have those two
things rise to prominence in the same country at the same time, and
then say the two circumstances have *nothing* to do with one another,
that they are merely coincidence, seems to me a ridiculous denial of
the obvious.

Martini & Rossi was late to the game when people began to make
the Martini cocktail with dry vermouth; the company did not introduce
a dry vermouth to the international market until 1900, and not to the
United States until 1915. But, by that time, the name of the drink would
have been commonplace, regardless of the vermouth brand being used.
(Perhaps that sense of losing control of its meal ticket in America fueled
those rather petulant Martini & Rossi ads in the 1900s.)

More than their American counterparts, European bartenders
have accepted it as common knowledge that the Martini cocktail
name is derived from Martini & Rossi. This was true even when cocktail manuals were published in countries with their own vermouth
traditions. A couple of French cocktail books from the early twentieth
century, including *American-Bar,* by Frank P. Newman (1904), name
checked the Italian vermouth for use in the drink (and not because
the brand was advertised in the book, which was often the case when
brands were specified).

In *Das Mixbuch*, published in 1953, German author Franz Josef
Müller felt no need to waste time with alternate theories. "In America
in the last century," the book said, "the vermouth of the company

Martini & Rossi was the most imported one. Until valid proof to the contrary, the assumption is that the Martini derives its name from the Martini vermouth."

The Martini Shot

How exactly did the Martini attain cocktail preeminence? When did it become the ne plus ultra of mixed drinks, the standard by which all cocktails would forever be judged? How did it become a totem of American culture, alongside apple pie, hot dogs, blue jeans, baseball, and a two-car garage?

Prohibition certainly gave the drink a boost. There was a lot of gin imbibed during those dry years. And President Franklin Delano Roosevelt, an ardent amateur mixologist, helped. A fan of Martinis, mixed them up at the White House following the ratification of the Twenty-First Amendment, and end of Prohibition in 1933, was a Martini.

But more people eating apple pie and attending baseball games don't push those things over the line from popular to sacred. That's achieved by outside forces. When poets, journalists, politicians, novelists, and artists began taking up baseball as a subject, that's when baseball became an American icon. So it was with the Martini. Americans were drinking plenty of Manhattans, too, but cultural beacons weren't composing odes to the Manhattan, so it remained just a drink. The Martini, however—oh, how strongly serious artists felt the need to have an opinion on the Martini.

This lionization began in earnest in the 1920s, when footloose expatriate members of America's Lost Generation latched onto the Martini as a symbol of sophistication, rebellion, American-ness, or whatever characteristics they cared to project upon the drink.

The prescient father of the literary Martini was Jack London, who made the cocktail the fuel that propelled Burning Daylight, the capitalistic antihero of his 1910 novel of the same name. Burning Daylight is the nickname of Elam Harnish, who strikes it rich in the Yukon gold rush, then moves to San Francisco to establish himself as a respectable robber baron. The regular intake of Martinis is part of his new persona. Wrote London, "Nobody seemed to notice the unusualness of the Martini at midnight, though Daylight looked sharply for that very thing; for he had long since learned that Martinis had their strictly appointed times and places." One of those times—as it is still today—is at the close of business, when "his everlasting call went out for a Martini, and for a double-Martini at that." London can safely be credited with the idea of the businessman who regards the Martini as his due at the end of a long day.

Few novels mention the Martini as many times as *Burning Daylight*. But future mentions would acquire more fame. Ernest Hemingway, as big a drinker as London, slipped cocktail cameos into almost all his works. The Martini appeared in his first novel, *The Sun Also Rises* (1926), where, in the final pages of the book, the central figures, Jake Barnes and Lady Brett Ashley, order Martinis in a Madrid bar. But Hemingway's most quoted Martini line came in *A Farewell to Arms* (1929), where, again, the protagonist, Frederic Henry, meets with his romantic interest at a bar and orders Martinis: "The sandwiches came and I ate three and drank a couple more martinis. I had never tasted anything so cool and clean. They made me feel civilized." Hemingway undoubtedly spoke for many when he penned that last line.

In 1950, Hemingway was still throwing Martinis down his characters' throats, this time in *Across the River and into the Trees*. At Harry's Bar, in Venice, Colonel Cantwell orders two "Montgomerys. Fifteen to one," for himself and his young Italian love, Renata (see page 99).

A lot of the seriousness that people, particularly men, attach to the Martini can arguably to traced to Hemingway's lionization of the drink. There is no American author more slavishly adored by his fans, who are prone to aspire to the sort of manly, high-adventure life they imagine the novelist lived. If Hemingway tended to weight the Martini with meaning, his contemporary and literary rival, F. Scott Fitzgerald, saw the fun in the cocktail. "We walked into the bar with that defiant feeling that characterizes the day of departure and ordered four Martinis," he wrote in his 1926 story "The Rich Boy." "After one cocktail a change came over him—he suddenly reached across and slapped my knee with the first joviality I had seen him exhibit for months."

Now-forgotten novelist John Allen Miner Thomas did Hemingway and Fitzgerald one better by naming his sole work of fiction after the cocktail. *Dry Martini: A Gentleman Turns to Love* (1926) told of an old libertine named Willoughby Quimby, whose life of pleasant dissipation and debauchery is interrupted when his long-ignored, now-grown daughter comes to visit him in Paris. Quimby's favorite haunt is a bar referred to as Dan's Place. Thomas—a graduate of Browning, Hotchkiss, and Yale and a member of Skull and Bones—appears to have enjoyed all the advantages of his class. He spent the summer of 1923 studying at the Sorbonne, and writes knowingly of Paris's drinking culture:

> Over the fair city by the Seine they sowed the hardy Martini, the fruitful Bronx, the sturdy Manhattan, the rugged highball. And Paris proved fertile ground. From the broad plateau of the Place de la Concorde to the pleasant slopes of Montmartre flourished the fruit of the sowing. Bar after bar sprang like alcoholic mushrooms among the drab cafes.

The final scene of the very slight and whimsical story has Quimby, back at Dan's and free of all familial encumbrances, ordering the title drink. The story was made into a silent film (now lost) in 1928, with Mary Astor as the daughter. (Thomas, one can surmise, inhaled a few dry Martinis in his time. He died in 1932 at the age of thirty-two.)

English playwright and composer Noël Coward, unsurprisingly, saw the Martini as an extension of urbanity, not too different from proper evening clothes or a cigarette holder. The sophisticated, quipping protagonist in his 1941 farce, *Blithe Spirit,* doesn't allow the sudden appearance of his late wife as a ghost to get in the way of cocktail hour. Fellow Briton, poet W. H. Auden, took a fiercer view of the drink, writing, within his poem "Symmetries and Asymmetries," the haiku

Could any tiger
Drink martinis, smoke cigars,
And last as we do?

No doubt, this is how many ardent Martini devotees think of themselves as they drain their third glass. Auden loved his Martinis deeply, and, to show that love, drank them often. On the one hundredth anniversary of his birth, in 2007, hundreds gathered at his birthplace of York, England, to toast him with a Martini.

For postwar American writers, the Martini seemed to transition from cultured accessory—a switch by which you turned on jollity and humanity—to security blanket—a depended-upon weapon against the encroachment of barbarism, melancholy, and change. The WASP-ish characters in Edward Albee's plays and John Cheever's stories retreated into the knowable comfort of their Martinis. E. B. White saw the drink not as a party starter, but as "the elixir of quietude." Food writer M. F. K. Fisher wrote in a 1949 article, "A well-made Martini or Gibson, correctly chilled and nicely served, has been more often my true friend than any two-legged creature." It's a sentiment I well understand, but a bleak one nonetheless. More optimistic was Elaine Dundy, who wrote in her picaresque coming-of-age novel *The Dud Avocado* (1958), "We had dry Martinis; great wing-shaped glasses of perfumed fire, tangy as the early morning air."

Simultaneously, movies did more than their share to plump the Martini's position in society. The most renowned cinematic appearance of the Martini is still, after all these years, *The Thin Man*, the breezy adaptation of Dashiell Hammett's detective novel about debonair husband-and-wife sleuths Nick and Nora Charles. The year the film came out is important: 1934. Prohibition was over and the filmmakers seemed intent upon driving the point home. The Charleses never stop drinking, and much of what they consume is gin and vermouth. Nick is first seen instructing bartenders how to properly shake certain cocktails ("A dry Martini you always shake to waltz time"). When Nora finds him at the bar, she asks for six Martinis, in order to catch up with Nick's intake. At a party in their well-appointed flat, trays of Martinis are perpetually passed around. The next morning, a hungover Nora asks "What hit me?" Nick answers, "The last Martini." The characters even drink cocktails in the movie's poster. (Martinis do not figure in Hammett's book, but then, Hollywood seldom honors its sources.) *The Thin Man* was a tremendous hit. If some Americans had forgotten what a Martini was during the dry years, they remembered now.

Martinis never left the cinema after that. The films in which they've provided support are legion, but a few stand out. In Joseph Mankiewicz's *All About Eve* (1950), Bette Davis's character uses Martinis to quell her jealousy and insecurity over the scheming Eve; it is the cocktail that feeds the famous "bumpy night." *The Tender Trap* (1955) finds Frank Sinatra in full swinger mode as a womanizing New York theatrical agent. His mod bachelor pad is equipped with a bar, where drinks are frequently mixed. In *Teacher's Pet* (1958), a romantic comedy with Doris Day, the hard-boiled newspaper editor played by Clark Gable shows himself to be quite resourceful in an unfamiliar kitchen. He robs an ice pack of ice cubes to mix a Martini. For vermouth, he merely shakes a bottle of Noilly Prat and rubs the wet cork along the rim of the mixing glass. He then strains the drink through his fingers.

But did any filmmaker know and love the Martini more than director-screenwriter Billy Wilder? In his very first film as director, *The Major and the Minor* (1942), he and co-screenwriter Charles Brackett had supporting actor Robert Benchley utter a version of what became the humorist's most famous line, "Let's get you out of that wet coat and into a dry Martini." (More on the confusing origins of that quip on page 32.) Tom Ewell prepares Martinis for Marilyn Monroe in *The Seven Year Itch* (1955). In romantic comedy *Sabrina* (1954), elderly millionaire Oliver Larrabee displays the ingenuity that made him rich by pouring his already mixed Martini into an olive jar when the last remaining olive therein refuses to be dislodged. But the prize for most Martinis consumed in a Wilder film goes to *The Apartment* (1960). In one scene alone, the lovelorn junior executive played by Jack Lemmon dulls his heartbreak with at least a dozen Christmas Eve Martinis, lining up the toothpick-speared olives on the bar top in the shape of a star.

Luis Buñuel didn't feature the drink in as many movies as Wilder, but he may have worshipped the Martini even more. In his surrealistic masterpiece *The Discreet Charm of the Bourgeoisie* (1972), he lets one character pontificate for an entire scene on how to properly prepare and drink a Martini. Buñuel wasn't spoofing such pretensions entirely. He was as serious about Martinis in real life.

The Martini was so in sync with the Hollywood mentality that it gave the industry an enduring piece of jargon. The "Martini Shot" is shorthand for the last shot of a filming day.

The Martini's place in music is harder to quantify, but it's there, primarily, as one might expect, in jazz. Paul Desmond, the saxophonist with the Dave Brubeck Quartet, and composer of the outfit's immortal song "Take Five," once described his sound as being "like a dry Martini." In "Scotch and Soda," the Kingston Trio's mellow folk hit from 1958, the singer compares love to being intoxicated, saying, "Dry martini/jigger of gin/Oh what a spell you've got me in." It found a footing in musical theater as well. Frank Loesser, who composed the music for the Madison Avenue satire *How to Succeed in Business Without Really Trying* (1961), had ladder-climbing hero J. Pierrepont Finch serenade his reflection with "there's that slam bang tang reminiscent of gin and vermouth." What greater compliment could an up-and-coming young man pay himself than to compare himself to a Martini?

Doggerel, Cartoons, and Quips

Another way artists helped the Martini infiltrate every nook and cranny of society is through their idle thoughts and doodles. An early *New Yorker* cartoon to find humor in America's favorite embalmer appeared in 1930, just five years into the magazine's run. A drawing by Peter Arno shows a plane about the crash into a cliff, while a man inside exclaims, "My God, we're out of gin!"

After that, Martini cartoons became nearly as regular a feature in the magazine as cat and dog cartoons. There were two standard setups: a businessman (or two) sitting at a bar, and a businessman returning from work. Both wanted Martinis. Perhaps the most famous came from cartoonist Henry Martin in 1975, in which a talkative man in an empty bar confesses to the bartender, "It was a very bleak period in my life, Louis. Martinis didn't help. Religion didn't help. Psychiatry didn't help. Transcendental meditation didn't help. Yoga didn't help. But Martinis helped a little." A personal favorite of mine, by Mick Stevens, came much later. A smiling chicken sits in front of a small Martini at Ed's Roadside Lounge, the street visible through the front window. It is clear why he crossed the road.

The cartoonists who cast these jokes out into the world were confident they were sending up a social reference understandable to all. Poets and writers operated with the same assurance. Some of the most widely recognized words on the subject of the Martini were thrown off lightly, but lastingly, by three of the reigning humorists of the twentieth century: Robert Benchley, Dorothy Parker, and Ogden Nash. Appropriately enough, the origins of these rhymes and quips are as disputed as any Martini origin story. Nothing about the Martini is learned easily, it seems.

Let's start with the earliest, and most famous: "Let's get you out of these wet clothes and into a dry Martini," uttered Algonquin Round Table wit Robert Benchley one rainy night in the 1930s. Or was it Alexander Woollcott? From the start, no one ever seems to have been sure of the joke's author.

Benchley is named as the source in a September 1937 column by gossip columnist Harrison Carroll. But Benchley went on the record in 1942 saying he didn't coin the quip. That was the year the Billy Wilder comedy *The Major and the Minor* came out. Benchley, who has a supporting role, can be heard delivering the line. Writers Wilder and Charles Brackett put it in the script, thinking it was Benchley's. When Benchley said it wasn't, they left it there, because it *sounded* like a Benchley line. (He followed it up on screen with "I'd offer you a whiskey sour but that would mean thinking up a new joke.")

The joke also appears in the 1937 Mae West film *Every Day's a Holiday*. There, character actor Charles Butterworth says it. It could be Butterworth came up with it, and mentioned it to Benchley. The two actors were friends. The script is credited to West, but, as others have mentioned, West was a known credit hog. Benchley's son Peter, meanwhile, said the joke was hatched by Benchley's press agent, who pitched it to a columnist.

In the 1980s, *Los Angeles Times* writer Jack Smith tried to get to the bottom of the matter in a series of columns. But he only succeeded in getting confused. One thing's for sure: it was a good line, as good as any the century had heard. And in Hollywood, good lines aren't left lonely for long, but are freely borrowed. That Wilder and Hackett stole the quip is certain. Bentley guiltily acknowledged the same. Maybe West stole it from Butterworth and claimed it as her own. Maybe Bentley's agent stole it from West or Butterworth or both. Maybe they were all guilty of literary larceny and the true owner of the line remains unknown. We'll probably never know, and little matter. The world owns that line now.

Benchley's colleague Dorothy Parker came up with something nearly as good, and just as dodgy in its history. Her famous stanza ran

> *I like to have a Martini,*
> *Two at the very most.*
> *After three I'm under the table,*
> *After four I'm under my host.*

Like Benchley's wet clothes–dry Martini bit, this piece of verse certainly sounded like its supposed author. And, like Benchley, Parker by reputation, was given credit for other people's witticisms. (When you're a professional wit, that sort of thing happens.) It has been attributed to her since the 1960s, though always without proof. Two drinks writers, Troy Patterson and Wayne Curtis, tried to crack the case recently. Patterson traced its origins to two sources. Random House cofounder Bennett Cerf quoted Parker, talking about a party, saying, "Enjoyed it? One more drink and I'd have been under the host!" And a 1959 college humor magazine from the University of Virginia ran the poem

> *I wish I could drink like a lady.*
> *"Two or three," at the most.*
> *But two, and I'm under the table—*
> *And three, I'm under the host.*

Nobody cares. Since the 1990s, it has been widely attributed to Parker, perhaps because Barnaby Conrad III put the poem in his popular 1995 book *The Martini*. The growth of the quote's reputation can be seen in that it's not included in the original 1981 edition of Lowell Edmund's *The Silver Bullet*, but is in the revised version that came out in 1998. It's included in *The Portable Dorothy Parker* (1973), which means that even Parker scholars don't care whether the poem is actually Parker's. In 2011, the New York Distilling Company of Brooklyn went so far as to put the quote on the label of their Dorothy Parker Gin.

Finally, there is a poem sketched out by Ogden Nash, twentieth-century America's reigning king of whimsical rhymes. It runs

> *There is something about a Martini,*
> *A tingle remarkably pleasant;*
> *A yellow, a mellow Martini;*
> *I wish I had one at present.*
> *There is something about a Martini,*
> *Ere the dining and dancing begin,*

And to tell you the truth,
It is not the vermouth—
I think that perhaps it's the gin.

Most people know it as a stand-alone stanza that goes by the name "A Drink with Something in It." But it began as a longer poem called "Prelude to Pleasure," with stanzas devoted to the Old-Fashioned, Mint Julep, Highball, and Wassail, as well. Nash appears to have written it for the Continental Distilling Corporation of Philadelphia, which published it in 1934 as part of a one-thousand-copy, limited-edition promotional pamphlet. Nash was in his first flush of fame then, and perhaps not averse to corporate contract work.

It might have been lost to history. But in March 1950, the *Chicago Tribune* and *St. Louis Post-Dispatch* published a poem attributed to Ross Hamilton, titled "High and Dry," which clearly stole lines from the Nash verse. Perhaps Nash got wind of this plagiary, because by 1952, newspapers were again attributing the poem to him. However, it was now called "A Drink with Something in It," and was down to one stanza. (Mysteriously, one Montreal paper referred to lines about beer and wine that were not part of the original poem.) The poem has kept that name ever since. Just as well. It's a better title anyway.

The urge to set Martinis to verse lessened as the century marched on, but it didn't completely die out. As late as 1979, Tommy Van Hecke, a bartending legend in his native Davenport, Iowa, offered the following poem to the *Quad-City Times*:

The Martini inception embraces every conception,
Like a twist of the peel for the executive wheel.
Or a very, very dry for the tipsy guy.
And a dash of sherry for the girl contrary.
Add a pinch of abuse with olive juice.
Oh, what's the use.
I work on the docks, put mine on the rocks.

The Martini Comes Home

Regardless of how many artists adopted the Martini as their muse, the cocktail would never have become a national institution in the years after the repeal of Prohibition if it had not been accepted into the bosom of the American home. It was. Men and women—who became acquainted with one another as drinking buddies during Prohibition—no longer needed to go out to get a Martini. They had all the necessary fixings and equipment at their disposal to make the drink themselves. The free market made it easy.

Beginning in the 1930s, department stores and specialty stores began offering all sorts of "Martini sets," which usually consisted of a decorative mixing glass or pitcher, a stirrer, two to eight glasses, and sometimes a tray. There were Manhattan and Old-Fashioned cocktail sets for sale, too, but the Martini set dominated. Following the end of World War II, production of the sets sped up dramatically. They were sold at low prices so that no household should be without.

That these sets were sources of pride for their owners was clear, and, over time, various models became quite elaborate. They were made from all sorts of material, including crystal, silver, aluminum, chrome, and wood. One 1955 newspaper column described one set as having "a container for the gin, an ice holder, a lemon peel holder, an onion holder for those who like Gibsons, and then the last, ultimate, final word on the vermouth problem—some like two to one, some like six to one, but in this kit the vermouth comes in a spray bottle." No other cocktail, in the buyer's mind, ever required or deserved so many tools to build.

These sets helped home bartenders master the Martini art. As Max Rudin stated in his 1997 essay "There Is Something About a Martini" in *American Heritage*, "mixing cocktails at home became one of the manly arts, like carving a turkey. The age of the middle-class Martini ritual had begun."

When the *Des Moines Tribune*, in 1955, profiled John Deere vice-president Marvin M. Schmidt as part of a series of profiles of local businessmen, it felt compelled to report—along with Schmidt's reading, political, and vacationing habits—the man's taste in Martinis.

Being a man of business living in the United States, he would have a preference, the newspaper assumed.

"'I'm a crank on martinis,'" Schmidt told the paper. "'I really enjoy a good one.' He mixes them 2-to-1, using special brands of gin and vermouth. 'I never drink if I don't know when dinner is going to be served because my limit is definitely two drinks.'"

Essayist Bernard DeVoto also rhapsodized about the Martini enjoyed at home. "The room quiet," he wrote, "the lamps shaded, dusk beyond the windows, and on the little table a big bowl of ice, and more vermouth and gin than we can possibly want. Whiskey if you say so, but why?—Marjorie and I have mastered the martini."

The Sahara Effect

The Martini's great midcentury heyday coincided with its marriage to the adjective most closely associated with the drink: dry. It's one of the many ways the Martini stands apart from all other cocktails. No other cocktail is so ordered. Nobody specifies their Manhattan, Mojito, Stinger, Old-Fashioned, or Gimlet be dry, wet, medium, or whatever. Only the Martini is treated like steak, with its devotees adamant about how exactly it be prepared. And like steak, for those fanatics, there is only one correct order. Steak: rare. Martini: dry.

"Dry" to the Martini drinker means "minimal vermouth." That has been its meaning for a good seventy-five years. But that is not how "dry" was first understood. In the drink's early years, "dry" meant a Martini made with dry French vermouth, as opposed to sweet Italian vermouth; or one made with London dry gin rather than Old Tom gin; or both. "Dry" could mean something as minor as not putting a dash of simple syrup in your drink; or omitting a cocktail cherry and using an olive or onion instead.

Hiram Walker could have intended some or all of these characterizations when, in the early 1890s, it began advertising its bottled "dry Martini." The same goes for Bellows Fine Club dry gin when it boasted, in an 1894 ad, "It has long been considered by connoisseurs as ideal for use in Dry Martini cocktails."

One of the earliest mentions of a dry Martini, by that name, in a cocktail book came in 1903 when *How to Mix Fancy Drinks* suggested, as a coda to its Martini recipe, "If a dry Martini is desired, use French vermouth." Frank Newman, in his 1904 work *American-Bar, Recettes des Boissons Anglaises et Americaines* (published in Paris), has a recipe actually called Dry Martini, which was composed of half dry gin, half dry vermouth, and orange bitters. Keep in mind, though, that, at the same time, there were recipes out there for dry Martinis calling for Old Tom gin and sweet vermouth. So the jury was still out on the accepted meaning of "dry."

Whatever its meaning, by the early 1900s, the dry Martini era had set in, leading to a novel and movie by that name in the 1920s, and many a lame newspaper joke about someone ordering the drink from a German bartender and getting three—or *drei*—Martinis in response. The *Pittsburgh Press* interviewed a local "mizologist" in 1904 and found him adamant on the subject of the dry Martini. Bartenders, he said, "ruin it usually by including syrup in the ingredients, and that is why the man who really knows what a Martini cocktail is insists on having it made 'dry.' Gin and vermouth, in their proper proportions, with a dash of orange bitters, is all that is required for the proper making of a Martini."

Cranks like that bartender would grow in number over the ensuing years. But it wasn't until the post–World War II era that things started to get a bit irrational, and that the eradication of vermouth became Job One for the self-respecting dry Martini drinker. Bartenders noticed right off. In his 1951 volume *The Bartender's Book*, Jack Townsend, then president of the bartender's union in New York, observed, "If the present trend in home mixing continues it will end up as gin drinking began—merely straight gin. The standard receipt for a Dry Martini among sensible bartenders calls for three parts gin to one part French vermouth. Actor Monty Woolley calls for four parts gin to one part vermouth in his. But Mr. Woolley's hair would seem to be all in his beard rather than on his chest compared to certain hard-drinking Westchester County suburbanites who ply their house-party guests with compositions containing ten parts gin to one of vermouth."

Indeed, bartenders who knew their drinks and their drink history didn't appear to approve of the trend. A bartender interviewed in the *Baltimore Sun* in 1958 shook his head and said, "Eventually the drink will have to turn back to what it was before. It's not an aperitif any more. People just want something to give them a kick. It's not even a Martini anymore." Another New York bartender of that era accused dry Martini lovers of being chiselers, simply wanting more gin for their money. Midcentury cocktail author David A. Embury recognized the movement as more of a pose than a preference, saying, in his book *The Fine Art of Mixing Drinks*, "This fad for drier and drier Martinis—for it is a fad as well as a taste preference—has been adopted by those who wish to advertise their sophistication."

A humor piece in the *New York Times* in 1952 went further. It wittily referred to the mania for dryness as "a mass madness, a cult, a frenzy, a body of folklore, a mystique, an expertise of a sort which may well earn for this decade the name of the Numb (or Glazed) Fifties." The dry habit was also satirized in Tom Lehrer's 1959 ditty "Bright College Days," in which the alumni talk of "Hearts full of youth/Hearts full of truth/Six parts gin to one part vermouth"; and in Malvina Reynolds's 1962 folk song "Little Boxes," in which the conformist denizens of the suburbs "all play on the golf course/And drink their martinis dry."

The style of cocktail was closely associated with the hard-working, hard-drinking American businessmen of the time, and, as the century wore on, with the idea of American capitalism itself. Columnist Art Buchwald joked, in 1957, that "State Department officials judge the progress of a country on how dry its martinis had become. No country was doing its share to defeat Communism unless the ratio of the martini was five to one."

This state of affairs led to a lot of "innovations" on how to achieve that perfect level of dryness. The "in-and-out Martini," in which the vermouth is poured in the mixing glass and then quickly tossed out, leaving a mere trace of its participation, showed up in the early '50s.

In 1955, a man named Eustace Scannell, formerly of the Alcohol Tax Unit of the IRS in Boston, invented a metal liquor meter, designed to accurately measure pours and cut down on spillage and waste. In a story that was carried in dozens of papers, he expressed confidence that his device would result in more uniformly excellent dry Martinis. "By having the liquor meters set on different gin bottles to pour larger or smaller quantities," he claimed, "you can make the Martini extra extra extra dry, extra extra dry, or just plain extra dry, as the customer chooses. Nobody ever asked for a wet Martini."

The American drinker's ruthless pursuit of the dry Martini also led to a cottage industry of gizmos to aid them in their fetish. Some of these inventions were created in earnest, some as a joke, and sometimes it was difficult to tell the difference.

Multiple companies manufactured specially designed atomizers to affix to vermouth bottles. This relegated the disliked liquid to the role of a misting. "It furnishes just the right thin fog for the truly dry Martini," promised the Arnold-Copeland Co. of Boston. Another brand was called the Mist-er Martini. A Christmastime gift box offered in 1955 by Solomon's, a Chicago liquor store, included gin, a jar each of onion and anchovy-stuffed olives, "lemon spray," vermouth, and a vermouth atomizer. It was called the Sahara.

There were other methods of dispensing vermouth in the most miserly fashion possible, many of them possessing a weirdly medical character, thus turning the home Martini maker into a surgeon of sorts. Vermouth droppers, which doled out the spirit drop by drop, were popular. Tiffany made one that looked like a small oil can. In 1967, Gorham Silver produced a "Martini spike," a silver-clad hypodermic needle that could inject your cocktail with the exact measure of cc's of vermouth you desired. It came in a box lined with green velvet, most likely to evoke the waiting olive. Cost: the 1967 equivalent of about $75. Most curious were "Martini stones," which showed up in 1959. The instructions read: "Pour just enough of your favorite vermouth into this soaker jar to cover the Martini stones. Soak for twenty-four hours. Place Martini stone(s) in a glass and add chilled gin or vodka."

The vermouth people came up with their own innovations. Beginning in the 1960s, Noilly Prat, hoping not to lose further business in the States, created a special dry, very pale vermouth just for the American market. When, decades later, in 2009, they tried to give the United States what the rest of the world was drinking, the Yanks still wouldn't bite. Noilly quickly brought back the America-specific version.

The Opposite of Sahara:
The Martini on the Rocks

At the same time that Martinis were getting drier and starker, they were also getting wetter and sloppier. A parallel trend, often forgotten (perhaps willfully), was the advent of the Martini-on-the-Rocks. You may have witnessed your parents or grandparents enjoy the drink this way and thought it an anomaly. It was not. And it is still not, even today, among the older generations.

"I would say 40 to 50 percent of the time, [customers] ask for Martinis on the rocks," said Mike Holmes, the beverage director at the Wickman House in Ellison Bay, Wisconsin, which boasts one of the best cocktail lists in the state. "Usually an older crowd enjoys them that way."

The Martini or Manhattan on the rocks is a habit picked up by Americans who came of age in the years following World War II. Adam Platt, restaurant critic at *New York* magazine, told me that, while his grandfather took his Martinis straight up, with a good amount of vermouth, his father preferred them dry and with "plenty of ice."

The Martini-on-the-Rocks began to nudge itself onto bar menus in the early 1950s. "Most popular cocktail seems to be a Martini-on-the-rocks," wrote Bert Bacharach in "Stag Lines," a syndicated column aimed at male readers, in 1953.

The elite on both coasts were lapping up the new style. The *Detroit Free Press*, writing about a new type of bar stool in 1952, talked of a time in the near future "when California sips its Martini on the rocks" on the new chairs. Meanwhile, sportswriter Red Smith, in 1956, ticked off all the earmarks of modern Gotham life, stating, "This is the New York of air-conditioned skyscrapers and television towers, of shrimp cocktails and Martini-on-the-rocks and filter cigarets [sic], the New York of Grace Kelly and Orson Welles."

By 1961, the *New York Times* observed, "As for Martinis, the two most significant recent developments are the trends to the vodka Martini and to the Martini on the rocks."

Gin brands were also trading heavily on the new fad. Gilbey's, Seagram's, and Calvert gins all ran ads boasting that their gin made the best Martini-on-the-Rocks. And they did not consider the drink a lazy man's Martini. "The perfect martini-on-the-rocks," preached Seagram's, "does not happen by chance, but by dint of skill and perseverance."

That hyphenated spelling was no mistake. Based on the way it was discussed in articles and ads at the time, the ice-bound Martini was considered something of a separate drink. It wasn't a "Martini on the Rocks." It was a "Martini-on-the-Rocks"—one word.

Today, the principled cocktail drinker might ask why anyone would debase one of the most perfect cocktails in creation by serving it over ice. Well, for many reasons. Ice, of course, makes things cold, and a Martini-on-the-Rocks is going to stay chilly longer than one served straight up. As Seagram's crowed in a 1960 ad, "Who said the Martini isn't a summer drink? Our good host above makes a martini-on-the-rocks that tastes fresh and frosty when it's 90 degrees in the shade!"

Detractors will point out that ice, while keeping the cocktail cool, also dilutes the drink at a perilous rate. Yet this, too, was considered an advantage at the time. You didn't get drunk as quickly. Furthermore, a Martini-on-the-Rocks is also quick work, and thus appealing to the home bartender.

It's also arguable that the on-the-rocks movement was yet another salvo in the postwar battle to banish vermouth from the Martini. That same 1961 *New York Times* article noted, "the die-hard drinker of the extra-extra-dry Martini has moved on to a straight gin on the rocks, a drink which, along with vodka on the rocks, has enjoyed considerable popularity in New York."

While the cocktail revival of the last twenty years has done much to erode the prevalence of the Martini-on-the-Rocks, the style persists at many rank-and-file bars and old-school restaurants and country clubs.

From Russia with Love

It is, by now, accepted wisdom that gin's grip on the Martini began to slip in the 1960s, with vodka taking its place; and that the shift was effectively nudged along by some very effective ad campaigns by Smirnoff and other brands. But, like many past offensives by Russia, this campaign was actually a slow and deliberate one that began way back.

As early as 1935, with Prohibition still clearly visible in the rearview mirror, Smirnoff vodka, in ads placed in various US newspapers, recommended readers try a vodka Martini, made of three parts vodka, one part vermouth, and orange bitters. A few years later, a Smirnoff giveaway pamphlet was promoting the same idea. It suggested, as a preparation, "Put 1 or 2 pieces of lemon peel with ice in mixing glass" filled with vodka and vermouth, "stir well. Strain into cocktail glass. Twist a bit of lemon peel on finished drink. Add an olive if desired." By the 1940s, even Walgreen's was stocking the stuff, its ads screaming, "Try Vodka! The Drink Sensation! Odorless and tasteless as a mixed drink. Ideal for Vodka-Martini."

Like Walgreen's, Samovar vodka, another popular brand at the time, knew exactly why this exotic elixir might appeal to Americans. And it had nothing to do with the way it tasted. In fact, producers all but boasted that their vodka tasted like nothing. "Because of its bland, neutral taste, Samovar Vodka—now available—is a natural for mixing many of your favorite drinks," explained a helpful 1946 ad. Smirnoff was a little subtler and more poetic about it, with their famous 1950s tagline, "It leaves you breathless."

By the 1950s, the columnists had caught on. "Café society's new cocktail fad is vodka martinis with black olives," wrote widely read syndicated columnist Dorothy Kilgallen. (The black olive thing, thankfully, did not catch on.) Kilgallen rival, columnist Walter Winchell, reported, "Smirnoff will ballyhoo the column's word-wedding in mags and papyri coast-to-coast: The Vodkatini." Thereafter he used the Vodkatini term a lot, either trying to popularize a phrase, as Winchell was wont to do, or honoring some back-room deal with Smirnoff.

In England, vodka Martinis had an additional connotation. The Associated Press reported that "London has a James Bond association where young people meet to drink vodkatinis—vodka martinis—in emulation of their hero."

The Spy Who Came in for a Cold One

This chapter will be short, because I find its subject such an irritant.

Since at least the 1970s, no journalist has gotten away with writing about the Martini without addressing James Bond. Often they begin their story with Bond. Because Bond, more than sixty-five years after writer Ian Fleming dreamed up the suave British superspy, is still the first thing many people think of in connection with the Martini.

It's a tiresome situation for Martini purists and persnickety drinks historians like myself, because, as any cocktail enthusiast is painfully aware, Bond orders badly, instructing his Martini be "shaken, and not stirred" (later shortened, in the films, to "shaken, not stirred"). I know, I know, the antisnobbery brigade insist that there is no wrong way to drink, just *your* way, and everyone should please themselves. But let's just say Bond's famous call for a "shaken, not stirred" vodka Martini does not result in the best Martini ever made. And his order's fame has caused many an unquestioning drinker to make a similar error, if only to sound smart and confident in front of the bartender. (It doesn't work. Trust me.)

Why did Fleming instruct his creation to drink thusly? It could be regarded as a trendy order for the time, with Bond staying ahead of the curve in the 1950s, when vodka was on the rise; or a sign of Bond's international lifestyle, given vodka is mother's milk to the Soviet Union, his chief opponent. (Bond did, for the record, order gin Martinis occasionally, but it is the vodka Martini with which he is most identified.) Or it could be Fleming, a heavy drinker, liked his Martinis that way, and projected his tastes upon Bond.

Or maybe it doesn't matter. Truth is, we've been focusing too much on the spy's Martini preferences. The fact is Bond drank a lot of everything in Fleming's books, from Champagne to whiskey to various cocktails. Martinis were just a small part of his liquid diet. In 2013, three UK physicians made a study of Bond's drinking in the Fleming books, and concluded he was a hopeless drunk who would have likely died at age fifty-six. That, as it happens, is exactly how long Fleming lived.

To Shake or Stir

James Bond wasn't the only person, fictional or not, to make a fuss over whether his Martini was shaken or stirred; just the most famous. This question of preparation has been raging for much of the Martini's life. Bartenders who have written cocktail manuals have fallen on both sides. The main difference, as far as I can see, is that the shaking advocates just instruct "shake," whereas the stirring apostles instruct "stir" and then give a lengthy defense of their choice, because the thought of a shaken Martini disturbs them so.

In his 1922 book *Cocktails and How to Mix Them*, published in London, Robert Vermeire notes, "The Martini Cocktail should be prepared in the mixing glass and stirred up. In America, however, it has been the fashion, since a few years, to shake this cocktail until thoroughly cold."

The Drinks of Yesteryear (1930) touted itself as "being the 200 authentic favorite formulas of a pre-Volstead 'Wine Clerk' who long smilingly served All Men and Yale Men and All Their Goodly Company." Its author, Jere Sullivan, said, "A Martini or a Manhattan cocktail *should be stirred with a spoon* [italics Sullivan's] instead of shaken unless the individual cares to have it shaken. (Results cloudy.)"

The American sage of the good life, Lucius Beebe, in *The Stork Club Bar Book* (1946), took up the topic as well. "A vast deal of pother has from time to time been raised over the almost fanciful advantages of stirring over shaking Martinis. The almost universal custom is for stirring them, but Marco, head bartender at New York's celebrated Colony Restaurant, makes a practice of shaking them vigorously and candor compels the admission that the only discernible difference between the two products is that a spooned Martinis is crystal clear while a shaken one inclines to a clouded appearance."

You may ask, if stirring is so great, why do all the characters in the movies shake Martinis? Because it's more theatrical. A bartender stirring a cocktail makes for a dull scene. You may further ask why many bartenders still shake Martinis. Because they are busy. Several bartenders have told me that they switch from stirring to shaking when the bar gets crowded. It saves a few seconds.

This book's stance is the Martini should be stirred, and not because it makes the drink colder, or some nonsense about shaking "bruising the gin." (Honestly, what thinking person ever believed that?) It's aesthetics and practicality. Aesthetics because—as Beebe and Sullivan pointed out—a shaken Martini comes out cloudy and storm-tossed. Shaking spoils the lovely appearance of the drink. Practicality because, unless you have juice or egg or dairy in a drink, there is no reason to shake a drink to integrate its ingredients. There's just no need.

There is a third method of mixing that seldom enters into this age-old debate. This is the thrown Martini. This practice traces its roots back to the nineteenth century when, in the absence of modern cocktail shakers and associated equipment, almost all cocktails were thrown back and forth between two glasses. Today, the throwing technique has found a home in some of the more theatrical cocktail dens of Europe, but is most closely associated with Barcelona. There, at Boadas, a small bar off Las Ramblas, many drinks are thrown, including the Martini.

The bar was founded in 1925 by Miguel Boadas, who learned the trick while bartending at the famed La Floridita in Havana, Cuba. Other bars in Spain, Europe, and beyond took up the practice afterward. The method is not just a showy flourish to dazzle customers. It leads to a genuinely different Martini, one that is aerated and lighter and softer in texture; it's not a bad way to enjoy the drink from time to time.

The thrown Martini is not common in the United States, but, if you'd like to try one, a couple of creative bars have adopted it, including the aperitivo bar Dante in New York's Greenwich Village, and Manolito, a Cuban-style cocktail bar in New Orleans.

A Glass by Itself

One cannot underestimate the contribution of the Martini glass in forging the Martini's mythic status. Few cocktails require specific glassware (the Old-Fashioned, Collins, and Mint Julep are in this class), but none have a vessel as famous or recognizable as the conical, long-stemmed Martini glass.

Answering how the drink came to be associated with its crystal home, however, is no easier than any other Martini-history question.

Author Lowell Edmunds found this out when preparing the revised 1998 version of his classic 1981 work, *The Silver Bullet* (retitled for the new edition *Martini, Straight Up*). In an appendix devoted to the Martini glass, he asked, "When was the stemmed glass with conical bowl first manufactured in the United States? When did it become associated with the Martini? Why did it become associated with the Martini? None of these questions can at present be answered satisfactorily." He added, "I will go further and affirm that any evolutionary view of the history of the Martini glass will be incorrect."

Among the various roadblocks to getting to any sort of answer on the matter is the fact that a stemmed, V-shaped glass "had been in existence for a long time and was a perennial possibility," going back centuries. It didn't come into creation specifically to serve the Martini. Another problem is that the sort of materials that might guide research to a conclusion—period glassware guides and the glass illustrations and photographs in cocktail books—are hardly in agreement. The vessels that look like Martini glasses to us were often labeled as something else, such as wine or Champagne or cordial glasses; and the objects that were called a "Martini glass" do not match our modern idea of that object.

"Martini glass" first emerged as a common term in the 1930s, after Prohibition was beaten back. But the Martini glasses that came out then took on all kinds of shapes. An advertisement for a curved Martini glass in the Honolulu *Advertiser* in 1933 explained, "The Martini glass has a deep bowl to make room for the olive. It should hold four ounces." A well-circulated 1934 ad for Fleischmann's gin showed a bartender preparing Martinis in small, round wineglasses. Another ad for Martini glasses, from 1943, depicts a small coupe. A 1946 article about an exhibition of useful objects at New York's Museum of Modern Art tells of "round bottom martini glasses in a greenish bubble glass imported from Mexico by Fred Leighton." A gift guide from 1956, aimed at brides, showed a "Martini glass" that was a flat-bottomed tumbler. The tumblers could be stacked for convenience.

One could argue that the classic V-shaped Martini glass wasn't universally accepted as the glass you use for a Martini until quite late, perhaps as late as the 1960s. Certainly, by the 1990s, when the Martini revival began, there was no refuting the connection between glass and drink. But by then, the vessel had taken on enormous proportions, and was more properly described as a "double Martini glass."

Some have pointed to the art deco exhibition in Paris in 1925 as the crucible of the modern Martini glass. There, Lobmeyr, an Austrian glassware company, unveiled its Ambassador series of glasses, created by Austrian architect and designer Oswald Haerdtl. All the glasses had a severe conical aspect, very much in keeping with the voguish art deco lines of the time. The glasses were very thin, but very strong. "You're not getting any taste of any material," explained Sarah Coffin, a curator at the Cooper Hewitt, Smithsonian Design Museum, who has made a study of the designs of the period. "It's like the liquid is on your lips before you touch the glass. You're holding an almost invisible drink in an almost invisible glass."

The exhibition traveled to New York and elsewhere, exposing Americans to the design. However, it cannot be assumed that anyone who saw the Lobmeyr glass looked at it and thought, "Ah, a Martini glass!" For none of the glasses, let alone the one that resembles a Martini glass to our modern eyes, were given names by Lobmeyr. In fact, that the series had a name, Ambassador, was remarkable. Lobmeyr typically just numbered its items. Giving a series a title was a nod to US sensibilities. "They recognized Americans like names," said Coffin.

Furthermore, Haerdtl designed that line without any thought of the Martini, because the conical shape goes across the board. It's used for wineglass and water glass and whatever. Even Lobmeyr itself does not claim authorship of the Martini glass, calling it "an ambitious theory with no real evidence."

In the past twenty years, it's become fashionable to knock the Martini glass as unwieldy and ungainly and prone to spillage. Cocktail snobs have campaigned for a return to the more graceful and manageable coupe. I'm with them in spirit. But that battle was lost before it began. You may see Martinis in coupes in the finest cocktail lounges. But 99 percent of the public expects that iconic bit of crystal geometry when they order a Martini, and 99 percent of the world's bars are happy to oblige them. The Martini glass, for better or worse, is here to stay.

Neon Nights

In 1951, a Canadian journalist who went by the handle C. M. B. wrote an article about driving through California. The writer bemoaned California's "wide-open state liquor law," and further complained, "Your eyes grow tired of the endless repetition, especially of one sign that has been sold by the millions to California barkeepers—a gigantic green neon cocktail glass with a fiery red cherry in its depths."

Twenty years later, Herb Caen, legendary columnist for the *San Francisco Chronicle*, who tracked the life of the city for decades, noted the same phenomenon, and wondered at the choice of cocktail. "The symbol of a drinking place in San Francisco is generally a neon cocktail glass with what seems to be a cherry in it, denoting a Manhattan," he wrote, "but do you know anybody who drinks Manhattans in this Martini town?"

The neon cocktail glass is a familiar image to any citizen, be it the sign that hangs outside some local restaurant or bar, or those seen in countless films and television shows. It is generally assumed that such signs depict a Martini. However, it appears that the manufacturers of the signs were flexible, and the colors of the glass profile and the round garnish within could vary.

Still, it may very well be that the Martini's connection with the conical, long-stemmed glass has less to do with the number of bars and homes that used that style of glass than with the number of neon-sign manufacturers who decided what that glass meant: Martini.

Like the art deco aesthetic that fed the design of the Martini glass, neon, too, came out of the 1920s, when the recently discovered gas was bent into the service of advertising by French inventor Georges Claude. By 1923, the United States had neon signs, the first ones adorning car dealerships in California.

Neon cocktail glasses began to appear in great numbers in the years following World War II, with many companies devoted to the trade. In the 1940s, newspapers were filled with ads looking to either sell or buy neon cocktail signs. The signs seem to have been especially popular in California. In his classic 1968 work of New Journalism, *The Electric Kool-Aid Acid Test*, Tom Wolfe wrote, "One after another, electric signs with neon martini glasses lit up on them, the San Francisco symbol of 'bar'—thousands of neon-magenta martini glasses bouncing and streaming down the hill." In 1985, a *Los Angeles Times* reporter credited a Cal State professor with the statistic of 4,884 drinking places in California. The writer added, however, that the number "seems low considering all the neon martini glasses visible in such cities as San Francisco."

By the 1980s, when Martinis had fallen out of favor, so, too, had the bright lights that advertised the drink. In 1981, a place called Georgie N' Co. in Cambridge, Massachusetts, was considered "tacky" by the *Boston Globe* because it had a neon Martini on its façade. Two years later, the *Chicago Tribune* opined, "Generally, a restaurant whose exterior sign promises 'good food' usually serves anything but. Add a neon martini and a blaring jukebox and you're talking potential disaster."

At least one artist of the time saw the iconic Martini sign not as trash but treasure. In 1983, sculptor Claes Oldenburg created one of his multiples, called *Tilting Neon Cocktail*. It was a continuous piece of aluminum tube, bent to resemble the outlines of a Martini glass, and set at an angle atop a stand. A green olive on a long toothpick was perched in the bowl of the glass.

"I had wanted a motive for this ubiquitous subject since 1954," the artist explained, "when I noticed that every bar in San Francisco was identified by an identical emblem, a cocktail glass in neon. This well-established sign for happy times is conventionally tilted as if the glass itself were intoxicated."

With the commencement of the Martini revival in the 1990s, the signs, too, came back into fashion. Owners of retro-style cocktail bars generally assumed that a neon Martini glass provided the appropriate finishing touch to their enterprise.

Fall from Grace

Among publications, the Martini probably never had a better friend than the sporty, overtly masculine *Esquire*. But by 1973, even *Esquire* had to admit that times had changed. The Martini, the monthly stated, now represented "everything from phony bourgeois values and social snobbery to jaded alcoholism and latent masochism."

A lot of ingrained symbols of American life took a beating in the countercultural 1960s: capitalism, the suburbs, suits, ties, short hair. Cocktails joined them in the doghouse, the Martini in particular.

The Martini's problem was that it was your parents' drink. And many young people in the late 1960s and '70s were having nothing to do with anything their parents liked, from music to morals.

Jimmy Carter didn't help matters. Among the most abstentious men to ever inhabit the Oval Office, Carter, while on the campaign trail, criticized the rich businessman's taxpayer-subsidized "$50 martini lunch," delivering the long-loved practice a knockout punch, reputation-wise. (Gerald Ford did not agree, retorting, "The three-martini lunch is the epitome of American efficiency. Where else can you get an earful, a bellyful, and a snootful at the same time?")

The Martini faithful didn't like this turn of events at all. The wailing and gnashing of teeth came from predictable corners. A headline on the cover of a 1978 issue of *Bon Appétit* asked, pitifully, "Whatever Happened to the Martini?" Writer Jefferson Morgan lamented, "Now I come before you with a heavy heart to ring the tocsin of the end of civilization as we have known it. The true Martini cocktail stands in jeopardy of becoming one with the passenger pigeon, the dodo, and the St. Louis Browns, a situation clearly analogous to the decadence of Rome shortly before the fall of the Empire."

The *Wall Street Journal* declared the end of days when the starchy Donald G. Smith wrote, in 1985, "The demise of the Martini is a sad thing and I hate to see it end with my generation. Not only is a grand old tradition dying, but our society is also losing something of nobility and character. The Martini is an honest drink, tasting exactly like what it is and nothing else. . . . It is a clear, cold, pure, honest drink—especially designed for people with established values and a liking for purity, even in their vices." (One can only imagine a young rebel's reaction to Smith's idea of honesty and purity.)

What was the Martini not, in Smith's opinion? It was not sugary. It contained "no egg whites, no black and white rums, no shaved almonds, no fruit juice, no chocolate, and no spices."

Little did Smith realize what was just around the corner.

The Return of Martini Guerre

The Martini's exile didn't last long. But when it returned, in the late 1980s, it sure didn't look the same.

"It seems that martinis are becoming more popular," wrote a puzzled-sounding Ann McDuffie in the *Tampa Tribune* in 1988. "Why else would Cajun martinis have become a hot topic of conversation?" McDuffie was referring to the creation of famed Cajun chef Paul Prudhomme. The Cajun Martini featured vodka or gin infused with jalapeño peppers, and proved a surprise sensation at Prudhomme's New Orleans restaurant. But that wasn't the only drink causing the columnist to rub her chin. "Now, there's the Japanese martini," she continued. "I don't know what it is 'cause I've just read about this variation on a theme. Maybe it has a drop or two of sake instead of vermouth. Whatever, martinis really must be making a comeback. Five years ago, the demand for martini glasses had declined to the point that the top crystal manufacturers had removed them from their inventories. Now, they say, there's so much demand for martini glasses and martini sets that department stores are back-ordered on them."

It was a nationwide phenomenon. A coast away, the *Los Angeles Times* reported the same year, "The return of the martini is more than a myth, more than wishful thinking of professional barkeepers. Wherever I've inquired, I've been told that there has been as much as a 25 percent increase in calls for the once ubiquitous cocktail that fell from grace several years ago." In Connecticut, the *Hartford Courant* concluded, "Despite its roots in the last century, the Martini has loudly emerged as a true end-of-the-millennium drink."

What happened? Some accounts suggested a rebellion against the self-denying trends of the 1970s (light beer, jogging and other exercise, health food). Others pointed to the Reagan Revolution, the ascendant conservatives bringing their drinking habits back with them. Some credited communal nostalgia for a more elegant era. As a character in a 1997 *New Yorker* cartoon said, "I love blue Martinis. It's like the fifties and the nineties all mixed up together." And, of course, vodka was still king, flexing its marketing muscle with flashier ads and fancier bottles. "The current martini boom," suggested the *Chicago Tribune*, "has little or nothing to do with the classic cocktail. The fire is fueled by the intense competition among vodka brands." Gin, too, wasn't without a few tricks. Bombay Sapphire, with its eye-catching blue bottle and less insistently gin-y flavor, was launched in 1987.

Whatever the reasons, however, one couldn't help detecting a certain Martin Guerre aspect to the revival. The Martini hadn't exactly returned. The "Martini" had. That's not just a snobbish way of saying that most of the new Martinis being served were made with vodka, though they were. Rather, it's that they were made with anything and everything. All you had to do was look at the menus at the new Martini bars to know that something was amiss. They didn't offer *a* Martini. They offered multiple Martinis, a full Martini menu, sometimes with dozens of selections. Nadine's, a joint deep in bourbon country in Lexington, Kentucky, offered a Raspberry Martini, a chocolate-flavored Lady Godiva Martini, and a Midnight Martini, made with Sambuca and red licorice. The forty-four Martinis sold at Déjà Vu Martini Lounge in Appleton, Wisconsin, included the Cloud 9, made with vodka, amaretto, Kahlúa, and Baileys Irish Cream. The Cosmopolitan, which emerged in the late '80s and became phenomenally popular, was itself considered by many to be a kind of Martini, though it was a sour and shared nothing, ingredient-wise, with the original Martini.

As drinks writer Gary Regan wrote in 1997, the Martini was no longer just a drink; it was a category of drinks.

Dick Lehr of the *Boston Globe* decided to get to the bottom of it. In early 1998, he filed a deep-dive exploration of the paradoxical trend to answer a few questions for himself, including, "Is it all junk?" and "Is there a point in mixology's continuum where a Martini is longer a Martini?" He concluded that the Martini movement was robust and in no danger of decline, but that, "like ice cream, there are 48 flavors, a crowded field that, to me, seems not to enhance but to undercut the martini point. The essence of the drink has always come across in the cold snap of the first sip, the immediate and heady realization that you are drinking booze, unmasked." The new Martinis were just "candy."

The best insight Lehr culled from bartenders was that much of the allure of these specious Martinis was the glass in which they came . Few drinkers seemed to care what was in their drink as long as it arrived in that urbane glass cone, a relic from another era that communicated "cocktail" to all who saw it. The glass was the thing, not the drink. As Jeff Benders, a salesman, told the *Lincoln Journal Star* in 1995, "It gives a man a sense of style. And that's important. I sell tractors."

Getting Dirty

"Clean" was the watchword for the Martini for most of the twentieth century. It was a sleek, see-through, unsullied thing. But as the new millennium approached, a cloud cast a shadow upon that silvery sea.

The *dirt* in a dirty Martini is brine, usually olive brine, but sometimes cocktail-onion brine. Bartenders started slipping a little of the salty stuff into the usual mix of gin or vodka and vermouth in the early '90s, when the "tini" craze was just beginning and an Anything Goes sign had been hung on the lip of the Martini glass. At first, journalists put the "dirty" in quotes to denote its oddness. By 1996, they dropped the punctuation; everyone knew what a dirty Martini was, because everyone was drinking them. By 1999, Tanqueray gin saw which way the wind was blowing; the brand's fictional mascot, Mr. Jenkins, sailed the seas in a yacht called the *Dirty Martini*. (He also

died in that yacht when Tanqueray decided to end the ad campaign. Jenkins' craft was reported to have capsized in the English Channel.)

Dirty Martinis weren't entirely a new idea. Brine made cameo appearances in Martinis throughout the twentieth century. A recipe for an Onion Cocktail in *Beverages de Luxe* (1914), by George R. Washburne and Stanley Bronner, called for three to four dashes of onion brine, along with orange bitters, dry vermouth, and gin, and a cocktail onion garnish. G. F. Steele, in his 1934 volume *My New Cocktail Book*, prescribed a drink made of equal parts gin and French vermouth; dashes of Angostura, orange, and Peychaud's bitters; and a teaspoon of olive brine. Franklin Delano Roosevelt, an enthusiastic Martini advocate who would shake up a drink at the drop of a hat, and whose product was said to be of highly variable quality, was reported to have splashed a bit of brine in his drinks at the White House. Because of this, many have called FDR the author of the dirty Martini.

If so, it took the public until the Clinton administration to catch on. But when people did, boy did they. Soon enough there were "very dirty martinis" and "filthy martinis." Brine had never had it so good since the day some publican decided to put a jar of pickled eggs on the bar top. But who were the people who drank dirty Martinis? Perhaps they were the same sorry souls writer Bernard DeVoto described back in 1951, who "in some desolate childhood hour someone refused . . . a dill pickle and so they go through life lusting for the taste of brine."

The protests of the Martini purist did little to discourage orders for the drink. Eventually, some bartenders tried an if-you-can't-beat-'em-join-'em approach, electing to improve the unavoidable cocktail rather than banish it. Australian barman Naren Young perhaps went the furthest with his Olives 7 Ways, created while he was beverage director of Saxon & Parole, in Manhattan. The drink had as many working parts as a Swiss watch, including an olive distillate, made by sending chopped Cerignola olives and neutral spirit through a small still; a custom olive bitters; vermouth infused with Cerignola olives; a bit of olive shrub; an additional spray of the olive bitters; a few dots of olive oil that rested on the surface of the drink; and a small dish of olives on the side.

A long way to go to dress up an intrinsically disheveled drink.

The Cheese Stands Alone

The blue cheese–stuffed olive is the dirty Martini of the garnish world, and its fortunes rose alongside its liquid friend.

Modern cocktail bartenders have done their best to bring back the lemon twist, or serve a better class of olive. But there's no question that the blue cheese–stuffed olive is the most popular Martini garnish on the planet. It's all you'll see at most steakhouses and other high-end eateries.

It's an incredible success story for a garnish that barely existed thirty years ago, particularly when you consider that the garnish field hasn't produced many classics. In the two hundred years or so that cocktails have been around, only a handful of edible accoutrements (cherry, pearl onion, mint sprig) have shown staying power, and most of those were introduced long ago.

Unlike the Martini it adorns, which has too many parties asserting parentage to mention, no one has laid claim to inventing the blue cheese–stuffed olive. It does, however, seem to have a home-town of sorts.

On January 14, 1994, a writer for the *Chicago Tribune*, reviewing a steakhouse called the Saloon, noted in almost blasé terms that "they plunked blue cheese–stuffed olives into Martinis." Nearly two years later, on December 15, 1995, the same paper interviewed a bartender at Club Lucky, another steakhouse, who said, "People come here for a martini, vodka or gin, straight up with blue cheese–stuffed olives. We stuff 'em ourselves."

Jim Higgins, the co-owner of Club Lucky, which is still open and still stuffing olives, told me that the restaurant has been dropping them into Martinis (three per toothpick) since it opened in 1989. "I wanted a house drink," says Higgins, who claims Club Lucky was among the first restaurants in Chicago to help bring Martinis back to the fore of local drinking habits.

Soon, the phenomenon broke out of the Midwest and, indeed, the United States. In 1999, Sydney, Australia, had them. In 2000, they were in the United Kingdom. But Chicago remained particularly obsessed.

On December 29, 2002, Chicago reporter Judy Hevrdejs delved into the stuffed-olive mania that had apparently gripped the city. "In that tiny territory long claimed by the cherry-red chunk of pimiento, martini drinkers can now find blue cheese or garlic cloves or jalapeño peppers," she wrote. "Or—and we're not kidding here—anchovies, almonds, asparagus, feta, mushrooms, or habanero peppers." Ami Franklin of the local Blue Plate Catering was quoted saying, "These days, at the minimum, we're doing blue cheese–stuffed olives."

No one at the *Tribune* carried the blue-cheese torch higher—or longer—than columnist John Kass. Kass told me that he discovered the treat in 1997 while lunching with politicians and journalists at Gene & Georgetti, an old Chicago steakhouse. "An older fellow ordered a Martini," Kass recalls. "I thought I'd try one. It came with two blue-cheese olives. And I was hooked." He let the world know. "Who was the greatest inventor in history?" he asked rhetorically in his August 19, 2002, column. "You might think it is the guy who dreamed up the Italian beef sandwich. Or the various creators of the TV remote control, blue cheese–stuffed olives, ESPN and so on."

A mere month later, he devoted an entire column to Marty Marcuccilli, who invented the Olive Express, a device that could stuff an olive with blue cheese in the blink of an eye. Kass thought him a genius worthy of a MacArthur grant. "You press it into a container of blue cheese, filling a short tube," Kass explained. "Insert the tube into the olive, press the handle, the cheese is injected. A work of art anticipates the toothpick."

Marcuccilli, a Chicago native, had a long experience with the fancy olives. As early as the late 1960s, when he was an executive with Zenith, he remembers taking note of the garnishes. "I spent a lot of time going to nice restaurants with people," he tells me. "That's where I came across them."

Higgins, too, recalls encountering the blue cheese–stuffed olive before he made them a Club Lucky specialty. "They weren't really common," he says, "but if you went to the right steakhouse, you could get them."

Stuffed olives as snacks are an old idea. In the early twentieth century, you could buy them filled with almonds, anchovies, onions, and the bright-red Spanish pepper called the pimiento. The latter, of course, made its way into the Martini early on, and remains the garnish most associated with the cocktail. Media mentions of anchovy-stuffed olives in Martinis appear in the 1970s, followed by a 1981 *Texas Monthly* report of jalapeño-stuffed cocktail olives, promoted by "Jalapeño Sam" Lewis, a notorious huckster also known for racing armadillos.

In 1971, there was a sudden craze for blue cheese–stuffed cocktail olives—but black olives, not the jumbo green ones we see today. "In San Francisco," wrote Earl Wilson, in "It Happened Last Night," his popular syndicated column, "the Black Olive Martini at Phil Lehr's Steakery satisfies those who want dry martinis. Ripe olives are stuffed with blue cheese and soaked in vermouth for two seconds— that's all the vermouth there is in a 'B.O.M.'" The drink spread to other bars and restaurants as well.

That brief sensation, however, seems to have been the work of California's olive lobby. Columnist Dorothy Oliver, writing in the *Chicago Daily Herald*, told how "the Olive Administrative Committee of the California Ripe Olive Industry" rode into town and introduced two new, stuffed-black-olive cocktails to the Drake hotel: the B.O.M. (which she misreported as "the Bomb") and the Black Eye (vodka, Dubonnet Blonde, and a gherkin-stuffed black olive).

Neither drink caught on. In 1990, however, blue cheese–stuffed olives resurfaced as garnishes at a Tennessee restaurant called Hibrows, according to the *Tennessean*. The phenomenon's trajectory beyond that is difficult to track. One thing that's clear is the trend built up a head of steam in the mid-1990s, just as the Martini revival began in earnest.

Brother Cleve, a Boston cocktail guru, cites the blue cheese–stuffed olive's natural home—the steakhouse—as crucial to the garnish's coming of age. "The idea of a steakhouse doing this first makes total sense to me," says Cleve, who, as a musician with various bands, spent much of the 1990s touring the United States and visiting its many bars.

His theory—a bit far-fetched, but not entirely implausible given the garnish's goofy history—hinges on the close proximity of blue cheese and Martinis in any given steakhouse. "Perhaps with the low-fat trends of the late '80s they weren't getting enough calls for bacon-

and-blue-cheese baked potatoes, so some forward-thinking GM or bar manager said, 'Hey, let's stuff it in the olives!'"

A New Dogma

In November 2002, *Esquire* magazine, backed by Tanqueray gin, sponsored a Martini-off. *Esquire* booze writer David Wondrich was the ringleader. His idea was to do "a real Martini contest" to remind the world, in the age of the "tini," what the cocktail was really about.

He invited any conscientious New York mixologist worth a damn to compete (there weren't many back then), among them Albert Trummer from Town, Del Pedro from Grange Hall, Shin Ikeda from Angel's Share, and Sasha Petraske. The young, black-eyed, floppy-haired Petraske had shaken up the drinks world a couple of years earlier by opening a signless, menuless, cocktail den called Milk & Honey.

Trummer won the contest with a very dry, in-and-out Martini that was easily recognized and appreciated by the judges. But the drink that left the lasting impression was from Petraske. He had absorbed all the information found in the old, out-of-print cocktails books he collected and knew that the Martini had once been a vermouth-heavy drink. He was also an iconoclast who likely didn't care much what *Esquire* or Tanqueray or the judges thought. He was going to serve the Martini he thought was good, and that Martini had more vermouth in it than all the other competing Martinis put together. Needless to say, it raised some eyebrows.

"Nobody could get a handle on Sasha's drink," recalled Wondrich. "It was the first time I ever tasted one. Nobody had been drinking 50 50s in years. That was just weird."

The battle lost that day led to an extended war, and, if the wet Martini didn't exactly win, it certainly put up a good fight, and continues to. The 2000s saw an amazing and utterly unpredictable comeback of the vermouth-y Martini. When Audrey Saunders opened her Manhattan cocktail bar Pegu Club, in 2005, she put the "Fitty-Fitty" on the menu—equal parts gin and vermouth, with a dash of orange bitters (see page 141). The media elite drank Pegu in deeply and soon embraced the Fitty-Fitty as their preferred rendition of the Martini. Within a few years, it was hard to find a drinks journalist who preferred the Martini any other way.

The bartending community took it up as well. It was a punk-rock move at the time. Gin was a hard-enough sell. But *vermouth*?! You were showing your true rebel bona fides if you drank that stuff publicly. No doubt, the bartenders and boozehounds liked the taste of the 50-50s. But the drink was more than that. It was a battle cry. It showed you were hip, in-the-know, wised up, had taste. It was a snob cocktail, maybe the ultimate snob cocktail.

How much did the 50-50 lovers love their 50-50s? Well, consider the reaction to a 2017 blind tasting of twenty-seven Martinis, held by online drinks site PUNCH. Among the judges were New York bartenders Thomas Waugh from the Grill and William Elliott from Maison Premiere, both of whom had made a close study of Martinis. (I, too, was a judge.) It soon became clear that the panel preferred a drier, more old-school Martini and the several 50-50s submitted, while appreciated, were banished in the first round. The thinking was that the 50-50 Martini, while a good thing, was a different drink altogether. When the results were published, cocktail Twitter had a meltdown. The 50-50 not a Martini? The 50-50 not a winner? Outrage!

The reaction was amusing and ironic, given that the 50-50 had only enjoyed renewed currency for a decade or so, and that its original reign as something recognized as a Martini, in the late nineteenth and early twentieth century, had been even shorter. Two blips on a screen dominated for a century or so by the dry Martini.

But then, the Martini inspires dogma. The Martini's history, it could be argued, is nothing but dogma, raving lunatics yelping from their soapboxes about what's right and what's wrong about *your* Martini. There is no difference, in the end, between the dry Martini martinet of the 1950s and the 50-50 zealot of the 2010s. They're both right—each is a delicious drink. And they're both wrong, in the idea that theirs is the superior drink.

The Martini Today

Aside from the return of the 50-50 Martini, the main story of the Martini's return to form in the early twenty-first century is how long it took. The ardent mixologists of the cocktail renaissance loved causes célèbres, and they had many of them. Any old drink that was in need of resurrection they revived, from classics such as the Old-Fashioned, Manhattan, Negroni, and Daiquiri to more obscure potions such as the Last Word, Jungle Bird, and Aviation.

The Martini, however, did not greatly interest them. They had reasons for ignoring it. For one, it did not need rescuing. No one had ever forgotten about the Martini. It was the last classic cocktail standing when they first took up the jigger and barspoon at the turn of this century. Also, there was that whole Martini revival of the 1990s, which produced a lot of unctuous "tinis," but not many good, actual Martinis. The injury of that period was still fresh in their memories. Let the Martini, with its many sins, sit in its corner for a while as punishment.

Eventually, though, some bartenders returned their attention to the drink. Again, there were reasons. The craft distilling movement has provided them with a raft of new gins to play with, many of them quite fine. Vermouth, too, has returned to respectability, with both new domestic vermouths and imported European vermouths newly available. Finally, orange bitters, once an essential ingredient in the drink, was back with a vengeance; there were two dozen brands where there had once been one (if you could find it). Between the gins, vermouths, and orange bitters, there were now so many Martini possibilities.

The final thing that brought the Martini back, however, was that bartenders and cocktail enthusiasts realized it was just stupid to neglect such an iconic and excellent cocktail. By the 2010s, a few noted new bars began to place their Martinis front and center, including Maison Premiere, Sauvage, Dante, and the bar at the Grill, in New York City. Many of the Martinis were of the dry variety.

And so, a new chapter in the Martini's never-ending story had begun. Its lesson: never count the Martini out.

The Recipes

There are no "tinis" in this cocktail book. No Appletinis, no Chocolatinis, no "tinis" whatsoever. Even modern "tinis" I like and respect, such as the Espresso Martini and Breakfast Martini, have no place here. The only recipes included are recognizably in the classic Martini family. The base spirits are mainly gin, sometimes vodka. No recipe contains juice or cream or egg or sweet liqueurs. If you want a blue or pink Martini, this is not your book.

The recipes that follow are either standard, recognized formulae for the Martini; precursors of the Martini (Martinez, Turf Club, etc.); similar cocktails that have ridden shotgun alongside the Martini for some or all of its history (Gibson, Alaska, etc.); modern descendants of the original drink (Martini-on-the-Rocks, dirty Martini, etc.); and personal recipes for the Martini by noted bartenders. Additionally, interspersed throughout this section are recipes for Martinis as they are made at bars and restaurants famous for the drink.

Following are a few guidelines on the basics of preparing Martinis, with tips on the equipment and ingredients you will need.

Equipment

I would recommend investing in each of the items listed here. Presentation and precision go a long way toward making a good Martini. It needn't cost you much, maybe $50 tops if you shop wisely. And the outlay will pay dividends for years to come.

A MARTINI OR COUPE GLASS (4 TO 6 OUNCES)

Use glasses with a smaller capacity for Martinis. If your glass is too big, the Martini will warm up when you're halfway through drinking it and become unpalatable. It will also be too powerful and prevent you from enjoying a second Martini. Always keep your glasses chilled, and do not remove them from the freezer until ready to use. If you forgot to prechill the glasses, a quick fix is to fill the glass with ice and let it chill while you prepare the cocktail.

A STANDARD MIXING GLASS

A pint glass can do in a pinch if you don't have a dedicated mixing glass. I prefer mixing glasses to cocktail tins, for the simple reason that you can see inside glass and keep track of how much you are diluting your drink. Also, contact with metal sometimes has an adverse effect on the delicate taste of a Martini. Many barware companies sell beautiful cut-glass mixing glasses. Naturally, these are more expensive than your standard pint glass; however, they are a beautiful addition to any home bar and add an elegance to the drink-building ritual.

A BARSPOON

A long barspoon (approximately eleven inches) is the preferred tool for stirring drinks. Some Martini purists insist on stirring with a glass rod, believing that contact with any metal harms the drink. If you can find a glass rod, more power to you.

A JIGGER

Most jiggers have a dual-measure design. Typically, they measure either 1 ounce on one end and ½ ounce on the other, or 1½ ounces and ¾ ounce. Modern Mixologist makes a very versatile double jigger: one end has a 1½-ounce capacity, and the other has a 1-ounce capacity.

A COCKTAIL STRAINER

Julep strainers, which have a perforated bowl, are for drinks made solely of spirits, which includes all the drinks in this book. However, a Hawthorne strainer, which is lined with a coiled spring meant to catch citrus pulp, will do the job as well.

If you want to get particular, and don't mind spending a little extra, I recommend the bar equipment put out by Modern Mixologist (www.themodernmixologist.com) and Cocktail Kingdom (www.cocktailkingdom.com). (Full disclosure: Cocktail Kingdom and I have collaborated on a set of Old-Fashioned glasses.) If you want to have a little fun shopping, antique and vintage shops, as well as yard sales and garage sales, are good sources for old Martini glasses and coupes of various designs and styles.

Ingredients

The cocktail renaissance has spurred an increase in the production and availability of quality spirits, liqueurs, and bitters. Most cities now contain at least one or two well-curated liquor shops that can satisfy a home mixologist's every spirituous need.

ICE

I cannot emphasize enough the importance of using good ice in mixing these drinks. Keep your ice fresh. If ice has been sitting in your freezer for more than a couple of days, do not use it in a drink. Throw it out and make a fresh batch. Old ice has absorbed other flavors lurking in the freezer. Also, if your local tap water is not of sterling quality, I recommend using filtered water or bottled water for your ice.

When making any of these drinks, do not be stingy with the ice. Fill your mixing glass nearly to the rim. More than any other cocktail, the Martini benefits from maximum coldness.

BITTERS

A dash is whatever comes out of a bottle of bitters when you upend it with a swift flick of the wrist. Be careful though: some bitters bottles dispense more quickly than others. In the past decade, the market has become flooded with orange bitters—the sort of bitters you need for most of these recipes. Regans' No. 6 is the most common. Some people combine Regans' with Fee Brothers to create a more well-rounded orange bitters (referred to as "Feegan's"). I also recommend Angostura orange bitters. You will also need regular Angostura bitters, lemon bitters, and Boker's bitters for one or two recipes.

GARNISHES

Garnishes are important. Just as much as bitters, they form a vital part of the cocktail. If you don't have lemons, olives, cherries, or cocktail onions on hand, don't make the drink.

Be sure your lemons are fresh and firm, with plenty of yellow skin from which to carve your twists. Wash all lemons before using them; they may be covered with residual pesticides and other chemi-cals. To remove the twist, use a peeler (a simple Y-peeler will do) and try to cut away just the skin, leaving behind as much of the bitter white pith as possible. Twist the garnish over the surface of the drink rind-side down to release the citrus oils, then slip it into the drink or hang it over the lip of the glass. Don't rub the twist along the rim of the glass, as it can leave a bitter taste that will inform your every sip.

For olives, Cerignola are recommended. (A good recipe for home-brined olives is on page 158.) I recommend making cocktail cherries and onions from scratch, rather than buying a jar at the store. There are many recipes for brandied cherries and homemade cocktail onions to be found in the internet. It is worth the effort and will greatly improve your drinks

Stirring and Shaking

"Stir until chilled" usually means stirring for about thirty seconds. Where shaking is called for, shake vigorously for fifteen seconds.

Early Martinis

For these drinks, the recipes are printed as they appeared in the original books, except where indicated. In addition, I offer tips on how to best interpret those recipes today.

Martinez, 78

Early Dry Martini, 81

Martini (Harry Johnson), 82

Martini (Theodore Proulx), 83

Sweet Martini, 86

Medium Martini, 87

Martinez

Jerry Thomas, *The Bar-Tender's Guide* (1887)

The 1887 edition of Jerry Thomas's bartending guide, which was published posthumously, contained a recipe for the Martinez, a drink many believe to be the immediate precursor of the Martini. Whether or not that's true, the histories of the two drinks have long been intertwined; it's rare a discussion of the Martinez doesn't include the Martini as well. Two ounces of sweet vermouth may seem like a lot, but the resulting drink is quite palatable. If you desire, you can reverse the gin and vermouth measurements; that works too. Angostura is an acceptable substitute for the Boker's bitters. For the slice of lemon, use a lemon twist.

2 ounces sweet vermouth

1 ounce Old Tom gin

2 dashes maraschino liqueur

1 dash Boker's bitters

Slice of lemon (lemon twist)

Combine the liquid ingredients in a mixing glass filled with ice and stir until chilled, about 30 seconds. Strain into a chilled cocktail glass. Express a lemon twist over the surface of the drink and drop it into the glass.

Early Dry Martini

Frank Newman, *American-Bar,*
Recettes des Boissons Anglaises et Américaines (1904)

Perhaps the earliest printed recipe for a dry Martini
appeared, ironically, in Newman's volume, published
in Paris. It's a fifty-fifty Martini with a few dashes of
bitters—the sort of drink that would become trendy
among the cocktail elite a century later. It's very simple,
and an illustration of what "dry" meant back then in
regard to the Martini. I suggest the orange bitters over
the Angostura. Newman is quite democratic in his atti-
tude toward Martini garnishes. Avoid the cherry.

1½ ounces dry gin

1½ ounces dry vermouth

3 dashes orange or Angostura bitters

Olive, cherry, or lemon twist

Combine the liquid ingredients in a mixing glass filled
with ice and stir until chilled, about 30 seconds. Strain
into a chilled cocktail glass. Drop an olive into the glass,
or express a lemon twist over the surface of the drink
and drop it into the glass.

Martini

Harry Johnson, *Bartender's Manual* (1888)

Two bartenders, two cocktail books published the same year, both titled *Bartender's Manual*. Again, we're talking Old Tom gin and sweet vermouth in equal pwwortions. The "½ wineglassful" in Johnson's recipe is equal to 1 ounce. Feel free to up that to 1½ ounces to make for a more sizeable drink. Gum syrup is made with gum Arabic and lends a silky texture to drinks. There are gum (or gomme) syrups on the market, if you want to seek them out. Or you can substitute simple syrup. Boker's bitters, disappeared from the market some time ago. There are a couple of re-creations of the formula available today. If you can't find them, Angostura bitters will do. For garnish, Johnson covered all the bases. Both the lemon twist or cherry work, but separately. The olive? Fuggedaboutit.

½ wineglassful (1 ounce) Old Tom gin

½ wineglassful (1 ounce) sweet vermouth

2 to 3 dashes gum syrup (or simple syrup)

2 to 3 dashes Boker's bitters

1 dash curaçao

Lemon twist, cherry, or olive

Combine the liquid ingredients in a mixing glass filled with ice and stir until chilled, about 30 seconds. Strain into a chilled cocktail glass. Express a lemon twist over the surface of the drink and drop into the glass, or garnish with a cherry.

Martini

Theodore Proulx, *Bartender's Manual* (1888)

Chicago bartender Proulx's recipe could hardly be more
direct. A Martini "is half Tom gin and half vermouth
made like any other cocktail; no absinthe." "Tom" is
Old Tom gin. I recommend Hayman's Old Tom. The
vermouth is the sweet Italian kind. Try Martini & Rossi;
it's what Proulx would have had access to. "Like any
other cocktail" is a shorthand instruction Proulx employs
often in his book, including for the Turf and Manhattan
cocktails. It refers to his recipe for a Whisky Cocktail,
which includes bitters, syrup, and a lemon twist, and to
combine the ingredients with ice and strain into a cocktail glass. For "1 part," measure 1½ ounces.

Lemon Twist
1 part (1½ ounces) Old Tom gin
1 part (1½ ounces) sweet vermouth
2 dashes aromatic bitters
2 dashes gomme syrup

Express a lemon twist into a mixing glass and drop it in.
Add the liquid ingredients in a mixing glass filled with
ice and stir until chilled, about 30 seconds. Strain into
a chilled cocktail glass.

Dry Martini
Barcelona

What better way to announce your allegiance than to name your bar after the cocktail you specialize in? Dry Martini was opened in Barcelona in 1978 by Pedro Carbonell. The bartenders wear white jackets. The small mahogany bar is only three meters long, and the original recipe for their house drink is written in big letters on the mirror behind it. The clubby room is full of bottles, banquettes, cabinets, artwork, and dark wood. Like McDonald's, Dry Martini keeps tabs on how many of its eponymous drink have been served. So far, the counter on the wall reads well over one million.

True to the bar's name, the Martinis made here are very dry, using just a few dashes of vermouth. When the bar prepares a Dry Martini, the bartender takes an ice-cold glass and places it on top of a silver tray. Each customer gets not only the drink ordered but also a certificate with his or her name and the number of the Martini being sipped. It's the only certified Martini purchase in the world.

Dry Martini

2⅓ ounces Bombay Sapphire gin

2 to 3 dashes dry vermouth

Olive or lemon twist

Combine the liquid ingredients in a mixing glass filled with ice and stir until chilled, about 30 seconds. Strain into a chilled Martini glass. Garnish with an olive or lemon twist, or both, depending on your preference.

Sweet Martini

Harry McElhone, *Harry's ABC of Mixing Cocktails* (1922)

The original sweet flavor profile of the Martini lingered for decades before the dry Martini finally achieved its status as king of the hill. Cocktail books from the early twentieth century are filled with recipes for sweet Martinis. Some contained two parts gin to one part sweet vermouth; some, equal parts of each; and a few demanded more vermouth than gin. Most were garnished with a cherry. For novelty's sake, I'm featuring one of the vermouth-heavy recipes, from Harry McElhone's book. Because of the large quotient of sweet vermouth here, I would opt for a more assertive London dry gin, like Beefeater. Use a good vermouth, with a nice depth of flavor; this drink is all about savoring the flavors of the wine. McElhone instructed a dash of gum syrup be added. I see no reason for it; the drink is sweet enough. The cherry, though, is a must.

2 ounces sweet vermouth

1 ounce gin

1 dash gum syrup (optional)

Cherry

Combine the liquid ingredients in a mixing glass filled with ice and stir until chilled, about 30 seconds. Strain into a chilled cocktail glass. Garnish with a cherry.

Medium Martini

Harry McElhone, *Harry's ABC of Mixing Cocktails* (1922)

Cocktail books in the early decades of the twentieth century often listed multiple recipes for the Martini, usually titled "Martini," "Medium Martini," and "Sweet Martini." A medium Martini typically split the vermouth, with an equal portion of both dry and sweet going into the drink. This is an easy-to-remember, equal-parts recipe. Plymouth gin works well here, producing a very gentle, soothing *aperitivo*-style cocktail. No garnish is called for, and it really doesn't need one. (If you're interested in experimenting, other medium Martinis of the day called for two parts gin to one part each of dry and sweet vermouth.)

1 ounce Plymouth gin
1 ounce dry vermouth
1 ounce sweet vermouth

Combine the ingredients in a mixing glass filled with ice and stir until chilled, about 30 seconds. Strain into a chilled cocktail glass.

Bix

San Francisco

When Barnaby Conrad III wrote his 1995 book *The Martini*, he knew his subject. He had experienced firsthand the dawning and zenith of one of the modern era's great Martini meccas. Bix is an art-deco-fever-dream club straight out of an Astaire-Rogers flick. But instead of black and white, the decor glows in shades of amber, gold, and moss green. A wide, graceful staircase with a silver bannister leads up to a balcony lined with lushly upholstered booths and banquettes. The long bar, carved from a single piece of mahogany, is framed on either side by two soaring pillars and above by an enormous mural, depicting a buzzing social hall not unlike Bix.

Bix was opened in 1988 by Doug "Bix" Biederbeck on a picturesque alley in the North Beach neighborhood of San Francisco. He opened it so that he and his Martini-loving friends, including Conrad, the son of a famous author, painter, restaurateur, and amateur bullfighter, would have someplace proper to drink. One of his missions was "to figure out how to get a Martini as cold as I could." He coveted the glass chiller at Jeremiah Tower's restaurant Stars, where he was a frequent customer, but didn't have the room for such a device behind his bar. He compromised by filling an enormous silver bowl with crushed ice. Upside-down cocktail glasses were sunk into it until needed. The basin quickly became a trademark.

The Martini glasses themselves were a principled choice. Biederbeck hated the triangular fish bowls then used at most places. He opted instead for a smaller, rounder coupe. "We took a lot of criticism, when the Martini boom hit in the 1990s, that our drinks weren't big enough," he recalled. "I absolutely stood firm. I said, 'Well, then have a second drink, because there's no way that a Martini is going to be the same drink at the bottom of a seven-ounce glass.'"

Most others, however, appreciated Bix from the start as a reservoir of bygone sophistication and respite from the harried, dusty world outside. When Conrad published his book, the launch party was, of course, at Bix.

Bix shakes its Martinis "partly for the theatrics," said Biederbeck.* "Customers rarely ask for it stirred. Also, it gets the drink the coldest the fastest. I know some purists think it dilutes the drink, but I think that is a nonissue if it isn't overshaken. We don't pound it at Bix. A few medium shakes."

Bix's Martini

◆————————————◆

3½ ounces Gordon's gin

½ ounce Dolin dry vermouth

Olive, onion, or lemon twist

◆————————————◆

Combine the liquid ingredients in a cocktail shaker filled
with ice and shake until cold, about 15 seconds. Strain
into a chilled cocktail glass. Garnish with an olive, onion,
or lemon twist.

*Doug Biederbeck personally prefers a wetter Martini.
His recipe is for four parts Hendrick's gin to one part
Dolin dry vermouth.*

Classic Variations & Kissing Cousins

There is a whole family of classic cocktails that are similar enough to the Martini to be forever categorized as riffs or variations on the famous drink. Yet, because they do, in their way, possess a personality all their own, they persist under their own name and have their followings.

Turf Cocktail, 92

Alaska, 97

Marguerite, 98

Montgomery Martini, 99

Tuxedo No. 2, 100

Gibson, 105

Martini-on-the-Rocks, 106

Puritan Cocktail, 110

Vesper, 112

Dirty Martini, 113

Vodka Martini, 115

Turf Cocktail

The Turf or Turf Club cocktail is a tricky customer. It and the Martini seem to have trod the same tipsy course during their early years, often crossing paths. Turf formulas often bore a resemblance to the Martini. And, like the Martini, Turf recipes were all over the place in the beginning, but usually called for some sort of gin and some sort of vermouth. By 1900, the recipe had settled down to something like the one here. Plymouth gin is specified in most of these recipes. For the vermouth, I prefer Noilly Prat. It gives the drink a bit more heft.

1½ ounces Plymouth Gin

1½ ounces Noilly Prat dry vermouth

2 dashes orange bitters

2 dashes maraschino liqueur

2 dashes absinthe

Olive

Combine the liquid ingredients in a mixing glass filled with ice and stir until chilled, about 30 seconds. Strain into a chilled cocktail glass. Garnish with an olive.

Musso & Frank Grill
Los Angeles

No restaurant or bar in Los Angeles serves more Martinis than Musso & Frank Grill, the old-school eatery that has fended off time and change for a century since opening in 1919. Nearly three hundred are sent out to patrons on a Saturday night. As befits an old standard-bearer like Musso, the Martinis are midcentury dry, with just a touch of Noilly Prat vermouth. Also in keeping with the joint's frozen-in-time ways is the house gin, Gilbey's, once a major brand but seldom requested today. (Gilbey's was also the house Martini gin at the Colony, in New York, another exclusive twentieth-century American restaurant of international renown.)

Part of the appeal of the Musso Martini is the presentation. The glasses are on the small side, by modern standards, but are accompanied by a small sidecar of backup liquor, nestled on crushed ice inside a hammered-metal caddy.

Truth be told, the Musso Martini isn't all that remarkable. But it is magical, owing to the environs. Even Ruben Rueda, Musso's long-serving bartender, recognizes this. "I try to make them at home," Rueda said in a 2017 interview. "I use the same ingredients. It doesn't come out the same. I think it's the environment. It's this place."

Musso Martini

3 ounces Gilbey's gin

1 barspoon Noilly Prat dry vermouth

Olives

Combine the liquid ingredients in a mixing glass
filled with ice and stir until chilled, about
15 seconds. Strain into a chilled cocktail glass.
Garnish with two olives on a toothpick.

Alaska

Jacques Straub, *Drinks* (1914)

The Alaska is roughly a century old, first appearing in cocktail manuals in the 1910s. How the drink got its name is not known, but Alaska was a hot news topic then, becoming a United States territory in 1912. Also, the drink is golden, like the ore famously mined there during many rushes. Never terribly renowned, the Alaska nonetheless became one of the "forgotten classics" celebrated by young cocktail bartenders in the early years of the recent cocktail revival. The big question when preparing an Alaska cocktail is the choice of gin. Though most bars make it with London dry gin, the earliest known recipe for the drink calls for Old Tom, a sweeter form of the spirit that was common in the nineteenth and early twentieth centuries. I opt for Hayman's Old Tom, as it makes for a more well-rounded drink.

2¼ ounces Old Tom gin

¾ ounce yellow Chartreuse

1 dash orange bitters

Lemon twist

Combine the liquid ingredients in a mixing glass filled with ice and stir until chilled, about 30 seconds. Strain into a chilled cocktail glass. Express a lemon twist over the surface of the drink and drop it into the glass.

Marguerite

Some cocktail historians like to tout the Marguerite as a major competitor of the Martini in the early years. Plymouth gin, in particular, likes to trumpet the drink's importance (mainly because the first known recipes for it, in Harry Johnson's 1900 edition of his *Bartender's Manual*, and in Thomas Stuart's 1904 *Stuart's Fancy Drinks and How to Mix Them*, asked specifically for Plymouth). But the Marguerite was never really a contender, appearing in far fewer cocktail books and news accounts. The recipe below is adapted from Stuart's. Certainly, it is one of the first mixes to resemble the sort of dry Martini the world came to know, using dry English gin and dry vermouth. (Johnson's version was much sweeter, with more vermouth, a touch of anisette, and a cherry.)

2 ounces Plymouth gin

1 ounce dry vermouth

1 dash orange bitters

Lemon twist

Combine the liquid ingredients in a mixing glass filled with ice and stir until chilled, about 30 seconds. Strain into a chilled cocktail glass. Express a lemon twist over the surface of the drink and drop it into the glass.

Montgomery Martini

The Montgomery Martini is a concoction of Ernest Hemingway, first introduced in 1950 in his novel *Across the River and into the Trees*. It is named, rather mockingly, after British field marshal Bernard Montgomery, who liked fifteen-to-one odds before entering into battle. Hemingway encouraged his friends at Harry's Bar in Venice—where some scenes in the book take place—to adopt these proportions for their Martinis. They did, and still do today (see page 122). The resulting Martini is very dry and very much of its time and author. It's also a pain in the neck, because who among us has the equipment at home to accurately measure fifteen parts gin to one part vermouth? Do the full 30 seconds of stirring. You'll want that dilution. Hemingway mentions no garnish. Either an olive or a lemon twist will do fine.

3 ounces gin

1 barspoon dry vermouth

Olive or lemon twist

Combine the liquid ingredients in a mixing glass filled with ice and stir until chilled, about 30 seconds. Strain into a chilled cocktail glass. Garnish with an olive or express a lemon twist over the drink.

Tuxedo No. 2

The Tuxedo, which drew its name, according to bar lore, from the same place as the evening suit—Tuxedo Park, enclave of the elite in upstate New York—is a confusing character. There are actually two Tuxedo cocktails running around, and have been since the early twentieth century. One, generally believed to be the original, contains gin, sherry, and orange bitters, and is bone dry. The other, typically referred to as Tuxedo No. 2, mixes gin, maraschino liqueur, vermouth, and absinthe, and is lightly luscious. Both are good, but No. 2 is perhaps more common. This version comes from Flora Bar, in New York, which does a great job with the drink.

Absinthe rinse

2¼ ounces Plymouth gin

½ ounce Dolin dry vermouth

¼ ounce maraschino liqueur

4 dashes orange bitters

Orange twist and cherry

Rinse a chilled cocktail glass with absinthe and discard the excess liquid. Combine the remaining liquid ingredients in a mixing glass filled with ice and stir until chilled, about 30 seconds. Strain into the waiting cocktail glass. Garnish with the orange twist and cherry.

Dukes Bar

Dukes Hotel, London

The Dukes Bar Martini is arguably the most famous version of the drink in the world. It is also unlike any other rendition. The gin and vodka are kept frozen and poured directly into equally frosty glasses, without dilution. (Dukes keeps several different brands on ice, so you can choose your favorite.) Just a smidgen of vermouth is added. It is, therefore, a pile driver of a Martini, murderously dry and cold, and so viscous it goes down like a glass of milk. Many have counseled not to drink more than two in one sitting; the bar itself permits only two. I would cut that to one and reserve an hour on your calendar afterward for recovery. The cocktail is prepared before your eyes from a rosewood trolley that is rolled to your table—a trick later borrowed by another destination Martini bar, the Connaught bar in London's Connaught Hotel (see page 108). Salvatore Calabrese, an Italian, gets credit for the Dukes Martini. The drink became renowned when famed San Francisco journalist Stanton Delaplane wrote, in his November 1, 1987, column in the *San Francisco Chronicle*, "Salvadore [sic], the bartender, makes the best Martini in England." (Calabrese was lucky to catch the writer's attention when he did. Delaplane died five months later.)

It feels somewhat irresponsible to recommend that a home bartender make a full 6-ounce Dukes Martini. So this recipe is for a half-Dukes. See how it sits, then decide for yourself if you can handle another.

Dukes Martini

3 ounces gin or vodka

1 barspoon dry vermouth

Lemon twist

Put a Martini glass or coupe and your preferred gin
or vodka in the freezer 1 hour before using. Pour the
vermouth into the frozen glass. Swirl it around the inside
and discard. Pour the gin or vodka directly into the glass.
Express a lemon twist over the surface of the drink and
drop it into the glass.

Gibson

The Gibson is commonly regarded as a Martini garnished with a cocktail onion. The larger story is not that simple. Onions were frequently suggested as appropriate Martini garnishes in early cocktail books. But the first recipes for Gibsons called for no onions at all, just dry gin, dry vermouth, and nothing else, not even bitters. By the 1930s, the onion had begun to sneak into the drink. By the 1940s, it had a permanent home. If you can, buy quality pearl onions or, better yet, make your own cocktail onions. A batch will take you 20 minutes and yield months of pleasure.

2¼ ounces London dry gin

¾ ounce dry vermouth

Cocktail onions

Combine the liquid ingredients in a mixing glass filled with ice and stir until chilled, about 30 seconds. Strain into a chilled cocktail glass. Garnish with a cocktail onion or two.

Martini-on-the-Rocks

There are recipes out there for the Martini-on-the-Rocks.
But let's be serious. This is a lazy person's Martini, and
I've never seen anyone put too much effort into making
one, let alone follow an exact formula. That's the appeal
of the drink, after all. No muss, no fuss. It's good to go in
a few seconds. I recommend olives as a garnish because,
again, I've never seen a Martini-on-the-Rocks served any
other way. A lemon twist indicates effort. Olives? Just
drop 'em in.

2¼ ounces gin or vodka

¾ ounce dry vermouth

Olives

Combine the liquid ingredients in a rocks glass filled with
a few sizable pieces of ice. Stir briefly, about 5 seconds,
to chill. Add an olive or two. Your work is done.

Connaught Bar

Connaught Hotel, London

The Connaught, a hotel in London's luxe Mayfair area, revamped its bar in 2008, bringing in two mixologists in the vanguard of their profession, Agostino Perrone and Erik Lorincz, to overhaul the drinks program. One of the immediate hallmarks of the new regime was the Martini service. And it was, indeed, a service. Taking a page from the nearby Dukes Hotel, the Connaught employed a Martini cart for anyone who ordered the drink. Each customer had the opportunity to make the cocktail their own by choosing from any one of several house-made bitters. The Connaught Martini quickly became a classic.

Since you can't really replicate the Connaught's bitters, create your own adventure by playing around with whatever bitters strikes your fancy. There are many brands and flavors available on the market matching the flavors offered by Connaught, including cardamom, lavender, and coriander. The same goes for vermouth, as the Connaught uses its own house brand.

The Connaught Martini

3 dashes bitters

2½ ounces Tanqueray No. Ten gin
or Ketel One vodka

½ ounce dry vermouth

Olives or lemon twist

Coat a chilled Martini glass with the bitters. Combine the
gin or vodka and vermouth in a mixing glass filled with
ice and stir until chilled, about 30 seconds. Strain into
the Martini glass. Garnish with olives or a lemon twist.

Puritan Cocktail

The Puritan, another old variation, lies somewhere between the Martini and the Alaska (page 97), using both dry vermouth and a bit of yellow Chartreuse. Brooklyn bar Tooker Alley serves a fine version. This is their recipe.

2 ounces Plymouth gin

1 ounce Dolin dry vermouth

2 teaspoons yellow Chartreuse

1 dash orange bitters

Lemon twist

Combine the liquid ingredients in a mixing glass filled with ice and stir until chilled, about 30 seconds. Strain into a chilled cocktail glass. Express a lemon twist over the surface of the drink and drop it into the glass.

Vesper

Ian Fleming and his creation, James Bond, caused the world to suffer many bad Martinis. But they also gave us the Vesper, a damn fine drink. Bond comes up with the recipe on the spot in the 1953 novel *Casino Royale*. Gordon's is a good English choice for the gin. For the Lillet, some people prefer to substitute Cocchi Americano, which is thought to have a flavor profile closer to the original. I am with those people. The spy's exact instructions to the bartender were to "shake it very well until it is ice-cold." But Bond was shake-crazy. I suggest stirring over ice. Either way, strain into a chilled coupe. Bond also asked for a "large, thin slice of lemon peel," as opposed to a regular old lemon twist. Does it make a difference? Hard to say. But it looks pretty.

3 ounces gin

1 ounce vodka

½ ounce Lillet blanc

Large, thin slice lemon peel

Combine the liquid ingredients in a mixing glass filled with ice and stir until chilled, about 30 seconds. Strain into a chilled cocktail glass. Garnish with a large, thin slice of lemon peel.

Dirty Martini

If you like your dirty Martini a little dirtier, add an extra barspoon of brine. For the garnish, feel free to add as many olives as you like. Olives are what this drink is about, after all. (A superstition that has trailed the Martini for years is that it is bad luck to garnish your drink with an even amount of olives. That is why you typically see Martinis adorned with either one or three olives.)

2 ounces gin or vodka
½ ounce dry vermouth
½ ounce olive brine
Olives

Combine the liquid ingredients in a mixing glass filled with ice and stir until chilled, about 30 seconds. Strain into a chilled cocktail glass. Garnish with olives.

Vodka Martini

I have always suspected that people who prefer vodka Martinis also like very little vermouth in their drink, because—as they've shown by their choice of spirit— they don't like the taste of alcohol. But I need a little flavor in my Martini, and since the vodka is not going to provide it, I advocate a decent dose of vermouth here, plus a dash of bitters.

2¼ ounces vodka

¾ ounce dry vermouth

1 dash orange bitters

Olives or lemon twist

Combine the liquid ingredients in a mixing glass filled with ice and stir until chilled, about 30 seconds. Strain into a chilled cocktail glass. Garnish with olives or express a lemon twist over the surface of the drink and drop it into the glass.

The Bar at the Grill
New York City

When the Four Seasons, one of the most storied restaurants in world history, gave its final service in 2017, the day was a hard one for people who care about New York history, fine dining, and Martinis. The landmark rosewood square bar—with its Philip Johnson–Mies van der Rohe–Eero Saarinen design, including the famous cantilevered barstools, crowned overhead with a metal sculpture by Richard Lippold—was long a haven for the well-heeled and well lubricated. It was a place where the urbane traditions of the cocktail hour were always honored. There was some concern about what acts of vandalism the new leaseholders, the Major Food Group, might inflict on the space. With a great sigh of relief, New Yorkers quickly learned that "respect" was the watchword in the bar's reinvention. The design was left intact, but spruced up. The bartenders still wore jackets. And Martinis were still the order of the day.

The bar was a perfect assignment for Thomas Waugh, whose original cocktails usually skew toward classical models. He focused on perfecting the Martini and its various popular variations. The house Martini is made with two gins (Plymouth and Tanqueray) and two vermouths (Noilly Prat dry and Dolin blanc). The drink is a taste of blue fire, dry without being silly about it and cold as the heart of a Wall Street banker. There was a kerfuffle among traditionalists when it was discovered that Waugh batched and chilled his Martinis in advance; they went from fridge to glass, poured from a chilled Christofle decanter, in the blink of an eye. I sympathize. Nothing can replace the sight and sound of a Martini made before you. But there's also something to be said for a Martini that is bracingly cold and gets to you in fewer than sixty seconds. And there's little argument to be made against deliciousness, however it is achieved.

The Grill House Martini

1½ ounces Plymouth Gin
1½ ounces Tanqueray Gin
¼ ounce Noilly dry Vermouth
¼ ounce Dolin blanc Vermouth
¼ ounce spring water
Cerignola olive or lemon twist

Combine and freeze the liquid ingredients for 24 hours
in advance. Serve in a chilled crystal Martini glass.
Garnish with a skewered Cerignola olive or express a
lemon twist over the drink and drop it into the glass.

Oddities

These drinks are forgotten tangents from the Martini timeline, drinks that never got much traction but are in the Martini family and, for the Martini completist, worth a look.

Allies Cocktail, 120

Benjamin's White Martini, 125

B.O.M., 124

Clarito, 127

Allies Cocktail

Hugo R. Ensslin, *Recipes for Mixing Drinks* (1917)

This drink's single deviation from the typical dry Martini
setup of the time is a couple of dashes of the liqueur
kümmel, which tastes of caraway and cumin, in place of
the usual orange bitters. It's a nice variation. The name
refers to World War I allies England (represented by the
gin), France (vermouth), and Russia (kümmel).

1 ounce dry gin

1 ounce dry vermouth

2 dashes kümmel

Combine the ingredients in a mixing glass filled with ice
and stir until chilled, about 30 seconds. Strain into a
chilled cocktail glass.

Harry's Bar
Venice

Perhaps the most unusual Martini in the world is served at Harry's Bar, the urbane Grand Canal–side watering hole founded in Venice by Giuseppe Cipriani in 1931. It comes in what can only be called a shot glass—frost-covered and emblazoned with the Cipriani logo, and filled with about 1½ ounces of clear liquid and a lemon twist.

The drink's appearance always startles newcomers, who expect the usual Martini glass. But Harry's has always done things its own way. The small glasses were originally employed because Harry's was determined from the very first to deliver cocktails as cold as possible—not an easy feat in the 1930s and 40s. Thus, small glassware, which kept the drink colder longer.

The preparation is singular as well. Dozens of the tiny glasses are filled with chilled Tanqueray gin and placed on a tray, which is kept in a fridge below the bar. When a waiter calls for a Martini, the bartender opens the fridge and pulls out a single glass. He then carefully ladles a barspoon of dry vermouth on the surface of the drink, gives it a brief stir, adds a lemon twist, and places it on the bar for the waiter to collect.

The resulting dry Martini is fifteen parts gin to one part vermouth. The Montgomery formula was a favorite of novelist Ernest Hemingway, who pushed it on Harry's staff in 1945, after World War II ended.

Harry's Bar Martini

15 parts (3 ounces) chilled Tanqueray gin

**1 part (1 barspoon) chilled Martini & Rossi
extra-dry vermouth**

Lemon twist

Pour the chilled gin into a mixing glass filled with ice and
stir for 15 seconds. Strain into a small chilled cocktail
glass—or a copious shot glass if you own such an item and
want to feel like you're in Venice. Spoon the vermouth on
top and give the drink a brief stir. Express a lemon twist
over the surface of the drink and drop it into the glass.

B.O.M.

In 1971, the Olive Administrative Committee of the
California Ripe Olive Industry decided it wanted some
of that Martini money and trotted out a concoction
called the B.O.M. (Black Olive Martini), which was
just a strong vodka Martini with a black olive instead of
a green one. A couple of columnists fell for it and wrote
the thing up, and at least one restaurant, Phil Lehr's
Steakery, in San Francisco, gave it a try. Needless to
say, the fad did not last. But, hey, there are people who
prefer green olives instead of black on their pizzas, so
might as well give this spin a go. The original recipes
instructed, in all seriousness, to marinate the olive in
vermouth "for two seconds." I've changed that to two
minutes. Let's give the vermouth a fighting chance.

3 ounces dry vermouth

1 black olive

Blue cheese for stuffing olive

3 ounces vodka

Pour the vermouth into a glass. Stuff the olive with blue
cheese and drop it into the glass. Let it marinate for
2 minutes. Pour off the vermouth, remove the olive, and
place in a chilled cocktail glass. Pour the vodka into a
mixing glass filled with ice and stir until chilled, about
30 seconds. Strain into the glass cocktail.

Benjamin's White Martini

Erik Bergengren, *Benjamins Cocktails Bok* (1931)

Twists on the Martini formula are numerous today.
Back in 1931, when *Benjamins Cocktails Bok* was published in Stockholm, however, they were quite rare. In
that volume, Bergengren gave us his dry Martini and
sweet Martini, but also his "white Martini," a novel creation asking for gin, white curaçao, bianco vermouth,
and orange bitters.

2 ounces dry gin

1 ounce bianco vermouth

2 dashes white curaçao

1 dash orange bitters

Combine the ingredients in a mixing glass filled with
ice and stir until chilled, about 30 seconds. Strain into a
chilled cocktail glass.

Clarito

Santiago "Pichin" Policastro, *Trágos Mágicos*, 1950

Santiago Policastro, nicknamed both "the Gallant
Barman" and "Pichin," was one of the most famous
Argentine bartenders of the 1950s. When you page
through his 1950 volume *Tragos Mágicos*, you won't find
a Martini. What you will find is the Clarito, which is basically a Martini crusta—that is, a Martini with a sugar rim.
In 2008, Buenos Aires bartender Federico Cuco redis-
covered the cocktail and launched a "Save the Clarito"
campaign. It worked. Today, you can order a Clarito most
anywhere in the city. The sugar rim disappeared, though,
and you'll basically get a dry Martini with a lemon twist.

The formula below is Pichin's original recipe and
instructions, complete with sugar rim. You can pass on
it if you so desire, or perhaps rim only half of the glass
in sugar. I suggest garnishing with a lemon twist.

3⅓ ounces dry gin

⅕ ounce French vermouth

Lemon slice for coating glass rim, plus
lemon twist (optional)

2 tablespoons sugar

These are Pichin's exact instructions: "In a glass shaker
or container that serves as such, place 4 or 5 pieces of
crushed ice, about the size of a walnut; then pour gin and
vermouth. Stir for 1 minute and serve in a glass. Before
serving, rub the rim of the glass with a slice of lemon,
dip it in a saucer in which a bit of ground sugar has been
placed, with the glass upside down, so that the sugar
adheres to the part moistened with lemon."

Personal Martinis

These are modern takes on the classic Martini, sometimes from particular bars, sometimes from particular bartenders, and a few from writers who possess an affinity for the drink.

Toby Cecchini's Martini, 131

Beefsteak Martini, 132

Gallaghers Steakhouse Martini, 137

Dale DeGroff's Martini, 138

Dante House Martini, 139

Sakura Martini, 142

Sauvage House Martini, 145

FAF Martini, 148

Trash-tini, 149

Bernard DeVoto's Martini, 150

Lowell Edmunds's Martini, 152

Barnaby Conrad III's Martini, 153

Toby Cecchini's Martini

Toby Cecchini is the owner of Long Island Bar, a beloved Brooklyn saloon housed in a perfectly preserved, circa 1930s, former diner. His formulae for classic cocktails are often rather involved and his Martini is no exception. For that reason, he wisely titled it "A Martini"—not *the* Martini, but a Martini—on the bar's menu. Hepple is an excellent new gin made in northern England in the classic model.

2 ounces Hepple Gin

1 ounce Dassai 50 Junmai Daiginjo Sake

½ ounce Lustau Vermut Blanco

1 barspoon Bergamot-Pomelo Tincture (page 157)

Combine the liquid ingredients in a mixing glass filled with ice and stir until chilled, about 30 seconds. Strain into a chilled coupe or cocktail glass.

Beefsteak Martini

Phil Ward, New York City

Phil Ward, one of the central figures in New York's cocktail renaissance, invented this drink while bartending at Long Island Bar, my local in Brooklyn. It didn't have a name when he first served me the cocktail. When I wanted to write about it, I pressed Ward to christen the potion. He came up with Beefsteak Martini. "Beefsteak plant" is an alternate name for the shiso plant, which informs the flavor of the cocktail. Ward refers to the shiso leaves as an "invisible garnish."

3 fresh shiso leaves

2 ounces Plymouth gin

1 ounce Carpano bianco vermouth

1 ounce Dolin dry vermouth

Place 2 of the shiso leaves in the bottom of a mixing glass. Add the liquid ingredients and let sit for about 1 minute. Meanwhile, rub the rim of a chilled coupe or cocktail glass with the remaining shiso leaf and discard. Add ice to the mixing glass and stir until chilled, about 30 seconds. Strain into a chilled coupe or cocktail glass.

Maison Premiere

Brooklyn, New York

As at Dukes and the Connaught, the house Martini at Maison Premiere is a production number. The Martini ingredients are brought to you on a tray, and the drink is prepared before your eyes. If you're at a table, one bartender prepares the cocktail while another poor sap stands at attention holding the heavy tray.

William Elliott, the beverage director at Maison, is a Martini fanatic, and prefers the dry sort favored in the mid–twentieth century. "There is much talk of the ubiquitous dry Martini of the 1940s and '50s," he said. "This is that Martini." Elliott uses Old Raj, a Scottish brand made by Cadenhead. A very specific gin, Old Raj gin is bottled at a strong 55 percent ABV and has a pale yellow tint due to the postdistillation addition of saffron. The vermouth, too, is particular, the modern artisanal Italian brand Mancino secco, which has nineteen botanicals.

The name of the drink, Old King Cole, is a nod to the yarn that the Martini's origins can be traced to the bar at the Knickerbocker Hotel, in Times Square. The bar was adorned with a large mural by Maxfield Parrish depicting the fictional monarch. (The mural now hangs in the bar at the St. Regis hotel.) The story is balderdash. But it's a nice name for a drink. Maison garnishes the drink with a sidecar of crushed ice, on which there are three skewered Castelvetrano olives, a well-manicured lemon twist, and seaweed. You choose the garnish(es) you wish and drop them in the drink.

Old King Cole Martini

3 ounces Old Raj gin

¼ ounce Mancino secco vermouth

3 dashes Angostura orange bitters

Castelvetrano olives, lemon twist, or seaweed

Combine the liquid ingredients in a mixing glass filled
with ice and stir until chilled, about 30 seconds. Strain
into a chilled Martini glass. Garnish with your choice of
olives, a lemon twist, or seaweed.

Gallaghers Steakhouse Martini

Dominic Venegas, New York City

Classic New York steakhouses have been, for decades, incubators for the Martini, making the cocktail by the hundreds when other bars and restaurants had given up on the established definition of the drink. Most of these steakhouses, however, were turning out Martinis that were watery, sloppy, insufficiently chilled, indifferently built, and made with bottom-shelf gins, vodkas, and vermouths. Gallaghers is a happy exception. When the restaurant—which was founded in 1927 as a speakeasy—reopened in 2014 following a revamp, management hired noted cocktail bartender Dominic Venegas to rethink the cocktail list. He brought the seasoned bar staff around to the idea of rendering classic cocktails with more finesse. Martinis are served in a smaller (but still sizable) coupe, rather than a mammoth Martini glass. Proportions are roughly three to one.

2½ ounces Beefeater gin

¾ ounce Dolin dry vermouth

1 dash orange bitters

Lemon twist

Combine the liquid ingredients in a mixing glass filled with ice and stir until chilled, about 30 seconds. Strain into a chilled coupe. Express a lemon twist over the surface of the drink and drop it into the glass.

Dale DeGroff's Martini

This is the winning recipe that Dale DeGroff submitted to online drinks publication PUNCH (punchdrink.com) when, in 2017, they blind-tasted twenty-seven recipes from leading bartenders across the United States. It's more than appropriate that DeGroff won. As the head bartender at the revamped Rainbow Room in New York in 1987, he spearheaded the cocktail renaissance in the United States. A classicist with the tastes of his generation, DeGroff's recipe is simple and dry, without bitters, and relies on a classic London dry gin, Beefeater. The only elaborate touch is the Martini Reserva Speciale ambrato vermouth, a complex, well-rounded option that uses botanicals such as cinchona bark and Chinese rhubarb. It is amber in color.

3½ ounces Beefeater gin

½ ounce Martini Reserva Speciale ambrato vermouth

Olive or lemon twist

Combine the liquid ingredients in a mixing glass filled with ice and stir until chilled, about 30 seconds. Strain into a chilled coupe. Garnish with a skewered olive or express a lemon twist over the surface of the drink and drop it into the glass.

Dante House Martini

Naren Young, New York City

Dante is an *aperitivo* bar in New York's Greenwich Village that specializes in lighter and low-alcohol drinks, day drinking, and similarly civilized European traditions. It is also one of the few bars in the United States that throws its Martinis, slowly pouring the liquid from tin to glass and back again. Throwing is a method that goes back to the nineteenth century and is still common in Cuba, parts of Spain, and a few other corners of the world. As you can see from the recipe below, Dante's Martini is a bit involved, with a lot of finishing touches. Aside from the fennel tincture, however, it's all easily put together.

2 ounces Fords gin

2 ounces Mancino secco vermouth

1 dash Bitter Truth lemon bitters

1 dash champagne vinegar

1 dash saline solution (1 part Maldon salt to 8 parts hot water)

1 dash Toasted Fennel Tincture (page 158)

Caperberry

Combine the liquid ingredients in a mixing glass filled with ice and stir until chilled, about 30 seconds. Strain into a chilled coupe. Or, if you're feeling athletic and adventurous, try throwing the cocktail. It's not as hard as you think. Garnish with a caperberry.

Pegu Club

New York City

Many bartenders in the early days of the cocktail revival harkened back to age-old recipes of the Martini, where the vermouth played a more dominant role. Sasha Petraske, founder of Milk & Honey on New York's Lower East Side, was perhaps the first to reintroduce this model. But Audrey Sanders, an owner of Pegu Club, which opened in New York in 2005, made the drink famous. Her "Fitty-Fitty" began with equal parts Tanqueray and Noilly Prat dry vermouth. When Noilly fiddled with their formula, she switched to the more delicate combination of Plymouth gin and the newly imported Dolin dry vermouth. For orange bitters, she used a house mix of Regan's and Fee Brothers—the only orange bitters brands widely available. The combination became known as Feegan's. ("With that in mind, you could also probably refer to this martini as a 50-50-50-50," she quipped.) Saunders is adamant that, since the drink is a mere three ounces in volume, only one dash of Feegan's is needed. "The Fitty-Fitty recipe is a lesson in calibration, so every aspect of it is dialed in," she said. "A lot of folks don't realize that vermouth can have as many or even more botanicals than gin does, and one of my goals was to pair them together botanically." Finally, she added, "a lemon twist is *absolutely essential* to making this recipe work. It sharpens the botanicals and ties it altogether. It's downright flabby without it."

Fitty-Fitty

◆

1½ ounces Plymouth gin

1½ ounces Dolin dry vermouth

1 dash Feegan's orange bitters
(equal parts Fee Brother's orange bitters
and Regan's orange bitters)

Lemon twist

◆

Combine the liquid ingredients in a mixing glass filled
with ice and stir until chilled, about 30 seconds. Strain
into a chilled cocktail glass. Express a lemon twist over
the surface of the drink and drop it into the glass.

Sakura Martini

Kenta Goto, Bar Goto, New York City

This is the house Martini at Bar Goto, a New York cocktail bar owned by bartender Kenta Goto, who was born in Tokyo. The drink, which has the novel garnish of a cherry blossom, was the first Goto created for the bar. "That's one thing I always, always wanted to do—use the cherry blossom," said Goto. "Everyone loves cherry blossoms. That's the national flower of Japan, too." That blossom as well as the addition of sake and maraschino liqueur to the usual gin results in a very delicate Martini. Salted cherry blossoms (the salt is a preservative) can be purchased at large-scale Japanese grocery stores or on Amazon.

2½ ounces Dassai 50 sake

1 ounce Plymouth gin

½ teaspoon Maraska maraschino liqueur

Cherry blossom

Combine the liquid ingredients in a mixing glass filled with ice and stir until chilled, about 30 seconds. Strain into a chilled coupe. Garnish with a cherry blossom.

Sauvage House Martini

William Elliott, Brooklyn

William Elliott illustrated his Martini skills when he unveiled the Martini service at Maison Premiere (see page 134). He cemented his reputation as a Martini master when he debuted the house Martini at Maison's sister restaurant, Sauvage. The mixture is unusual, using unfamiliar ingredients, but the result is recognizably a Martini, even in its sui generis way. The gin is Xoriguer Gin de Mahon, a Spanish gin loaded with juniper and only juniper. Subbing for the vermouth is Luli Moscato Chinato, a hard-to-find, high-quality aromatized wine, which Sauvage itself sometimes runs out of. Combined with orange bitters, the two ingredients are a bewitching blend. Mahon is fairly easy to locate. Luli is not. If you can't secure a bottle, buy a plane ticket to New York. (Though Luli is critical to this recipe, Elliott suggested that an acceptable substitute, in a pinch, is L. N. Mattei's Cap Corse blanc, a Corsican aperitif.) Sauvage garnishes the drink with an array of aromatics, but you can get by with just a lemon twist.

2¾ ounces Xoriguer Gin de Mahon gin

¾ ounce Luli Moscato Chinato

3 dashes orange bitters

Caperberries, nasturtium blossom, juniper sprig, and lemon twist

Combine the liquid ingredients in a mixing glass filled with ice and stir until chilled, about 30 seconds. Strain into a chilled coupe. Garnish with caperberries, a nasturtium blossom, a juniper sprig, and a lemon twist.

Tongue-Cut Sparrow

Houston

Tongue-Cut Sparrow is the most traditional cocktail bar opened by Houston drinks mogul Bobby Heugel. Thus, the Martini has found a natural home there. The drink can be had in a wet version—with two parts gin to one part vermouth, and orange bitters—or a very circa-1950s dry version made in what Heugel calls the Japanese style, wherein the ice is "washed" with vermouth, tossed, and then supplanted by two and a half ounces of gin and no bitters. "Japanese Martinis are bold, dry and very juniper-forward," he said. The drink arrives frosty cold and pulls no punches.

Tongue-Cut Sparrow Martini

¾ ounce Noilly Prat dry Vermouth

2½ ounces Tanqueray gin

Olive or lemon twist

Pour the vermouth into a mixing glass filled with ice. Stir
briefly, about 10 seconds, and drain it out of the glass.
Add the gin and stir until chilled, about 15 seconds.
Strain into a chilled cocktail glass. Garnish with an olive
or express a lemon twist over the surface of the drink
and drop it into the glass.

FAF Martini

Jim Kearns, Slowly Shirley, New York City

Burrough's Reserve was launched by Beefeater's master distiller, Desmond Payne, as a sort of sipping gin. Supposedly based on an old recipe by Beefeater founder James Burrough, it stands apart from standard Beefeater gin because it is distilled in small copper stills and rests for a while in Jean de Lillet casks. Bartender Jim Kearns found a place for the premium gin in the house Martini at Slowly Shirley, his swank, subterranean cocktail cove in Greenwich Village. The main two-to-one recipe is simplicity itself. But the recipe for the special olives is not. If you'd rather not bother making the olives, a lemon twist is an option here.

2 ounces Beefeater Burrough's Reserve

1 ounce Dolin dry vermouth

House-Brined Olive (page 158) or lemon twist

Combine the liquid ingredients in a mixing glass filled with ice and stir until chilled, about 30 seconds. Strain into a chilled coupe. Garnish with an olive or lemon twist.

Trash-tini

Christine Wiseman, Broken Shaker, Los Angeles

The Broker Shaker bars strike an amazing balance between casual and exacting. The atmosphere is laid-back and careless, and the drinks seem cheeky on the surface. However, each cocktail is precisely devised. The Trash-tini is a good example of this yin and yang. The name telegraphs a goofy send-up of the dirty Martini. But, as this recipe shows, the road to that spoof is a complex one, with multiple layers of flavor and execution. It's one of the better high-low-concept cocktails I've encountered.

¾ ounce Plymouth gin

¾ ounce Grey Goose vodka

¾ ounce Luxardo bitter bianco

¾ ounce Charred Onion–Infused
Dry Vermouth (page 157)

2 dashes Bittermens Orchard Street
celery shrub

2 dashes sherry vinegar

Cocktail onion and olive

Combine the liquid ingredients in a mixing glass filled with ice and stir until chilled, about 30 seconds. Strain into a rocks glass filled with a few large ice cubes. Garnish with a cocktail onion and olive on a toothpick.

Bernard DeVoto's Martini

Bernard DeVoto, *The Hour* (1951)

Bernard DeVoto, in his book-length rant about the cocktail, *The Hour*, declared that the only proportions for a correct Martini were 3.7 parts gin to 1 part vermouth. The man had his ideas. He also, in one of his most bone-headed exhortations, maintained that a Martini should be made with American-made gin. "Whatever imported gin may be for, it isn't for Martinis," he wrote. So much for London dry gin. Was a man ever more proudly wrong? But, in deference to his passion for the Martini, we're going to honor his preference. Luckily for us, there are many more quality domestic gins on the market now than in Bernard's day, ones that can go head to head with a classic London dry gin. For his 3.7 to 1 formula, I heartily recommend Dorothy Parker gin out of Brooklyn for a solid, stoic, and stiff Martini that even DeVoto would admire. Also recommended: J. Rieger Midwest dry gin from Missouri and Woody Creek gin from Colorado. As for measuring out 3.7 ounces of gin, just eyeball it. DeVoto says you can hum while you stir the drink, but not whistle or sing. Bitters are forbidden by the man.

3.7 ounces gin

1 ounce dry vermouth

Lemon twist

Combine the liquid ingredients in a mixing glass filled with ice and stir until chilled, about 30 seconds. Express a lemon twist over the surface of the drink, but do *not* drop it into the glass, or the ghost of DeVoto will visit your home bar and frown at you.

Lowell Edmunds's Martini

In 1981, this Rutgers classics professor published *The Silver Bullet*, a meticulously researched book-length study of the Martini's place in world culture. Thus, he established himself as one of the leading Martini authorities of all time. This is his recipe for a Martini. As you might imagine, it is very detailed and particular. I print his instructions verbatim.

2 ounces Greenhook Ginsmiths gin or Beefeater gin

⅛ ounce (for very dry) or ¼ ounce (for less dry) Dolin dry vermouth

Lemon twist

"If you do not have a Martini glass in your freezer, put ice cubes in the glass. The ice should be made with filtered water or bottled spring water. For the twist, wash the lemon skin with hot water. Then (1) use a paring knife to cut off a small slice to be twisted over the surface of the drink; and (2) use a zester or vegetable peeler to cut off a thin narrow strip to be tossed in the drink. Stir the gin and vermouth, preferably with a glass stirring rod, in a glass container with ice. All contact with metal is to be avoided. Dump ice cubes out of glass. Pour Martini into glass. Twist the slice of lemon, yellow side down, over the surface of the drink, extruding dots of oil. Discard the slice. Toss in the thin narrow strip, the ornamental twist."

Barnaby Conrad III's Martini

Barnaby Conrad III, *The Martini* (1995)

Like Lowell Edmunds, Conrad published an influential book on the cocktail. His recipe for a Martini is even more specific, and more fanciful, beginning with a paraphrased quote from Shakespeare's *Henry VI, Part II*.

---

5 parts (2½ ounces) Plymouth or Beefeater gin

1 part (½ ounce) Noilly Prat or Martini & Rossi dry vermouth

"First, kill all the lawyers, turn off your cell phone, and put a classic Dave Brubeck album on the sound system. It's evening and the sound of a piano is good for you. Maybe Paul Desmond will join Dave with a riff on his sax. Paul once said that he was trying to 'sound like a dry Martini.'

"I always keep two Martini glasses in my freezer so they're ice-cold when I set them on the bar. Drop a big handful of very hard ice into a silver shaker. Grab a bottle of gin and pour in enough for at least two Martinis, one for you and one for a friend. If you don't have a friend, the second Martini will be even more welcome.

"I like vermouth—and occasionally drink it on the rocks as an apéritif—so I enjoy a fairly wet martini. Mix gin to vermouth at a 5 to 1 ratio. Shake the hell out of it and pour. The ice crystals will turn your glass into the adult equivalent of a snow globe.

"Your day may be over, but your evening is just beginning, and there's always a moon in the sky."

Epilogue: My Martini

What is my Martini? I've wrestled with this question since I began writing this book. I knew I would have to weigh in on the matter at some point. And I really did think hard about what my ideal Martini was. What is it made of? How is it made? How is it served? I had plenty of ideas and did plenty of experimenting, tasting dozens of Martinis at home, using different combinations of gin, vermouth, and bitters and varying techniques.

But, in the end, it all began to feel foolish. An ideal Martini? A single Martini that I would drink until I die, eschewing all others? It was ridiculous, foolhardy. I would be denying myself so much, for there are so many great Martinis out there. That is the truth of the matter. There is no one perfect recipe. Instead, there are many wonderful recipes. I know. I have sampled a lot of them.

Certainly, there are Martinis I prefer, gins I prefer, vermouths I prefer; as well as gins I abhor, vermouths I abhor, and drink-making practices I abhor—such as not chilling a drink enough or leaving a sloppy ice floe of shavings on the surface of the cocktail. But the truth is, there are many more things I like than dislike. What would, for instance, be my gin of choice? Beefeater? Excellent selection, a benchmark London Dry. Plymouth? Also excellent, but gentler and completely different from Beefeater. Tanqueray? Strong and assertive. Bombay? Dependable and steady. Old Raj? Eccentric, yet fascinating. So many good gins. The same goes for vermouth. Sometimes I want something elegant, like Dolin. Sometimes I want something traditional and straightforward, like Noilly Prat.

Writers of the past who, in their books and articles, insisted there was but one proper Martini were fools, and it's a wonder that we've spent so much time analyzing their self-important attitudinizing. Bernard DeVoto and David Embury, while good writers and interesting thinkers, were doctrinaire pedants. They had much wisdom to dispense, but, when it came to recipes, they were cranks—and that's partly why we cocktail nuts love them so much. (Wouldn't you know it: DeVoto and Embury disagreed with each other on matters Martini.) Great Martini recipes differ, but they all rest within certain parameters, they all live in Martini-ville. They all answer to a certain profile that we, even from a distance and without our glasses, recognize as the drink in question.

So, then, what *is* my Martini? The recipe I give you on the following page is just one that has dependably pleased me over the years. I'm not saying it's the best Martini. I'm not saying it's my favorite Martini. I'm saying it's a Martini that never lets me down and always makes me giddy with anticipation when I know it's in my future. It is made with an obscure gin, Blue gin, distilled by an Austrian named Hans Reisetbauer, who is best known for his exquisite eau-de-vie. His gin uses twenty-seven botanicals from ten countries, but is far from busy in flavor. It is only made once a year in small batches. I am not choosing this gin to be a fancy-pants. I'm choosing it because every time I have tasted it, since my first sip at Tabla—the Danny Meyer–run Indian restaurant that used to inhabit Union Square, in New York—it has struck me as exceptional. I don't enjoy it often, because it is expensive and not easy to find, so I often save this Martini for special occasions, or when I feel like treating myself well. For all these reasons, I am happy to call this my Martini. But I will never call it my only Martini.

My Martini

2¼ ounces Blue gin
¾ ounce Dolin dry vermouth
1 dash orange bitters
Lemon twist

Combine all of the liquid ingredients in a mixing glass filled with ice and stir until very cold, about 30 seconds. Strain into a chilled cocktail glass. Express the lemon twist over the surface of the drink and drop it into the glass.

Other Martinis I like and make often:

2¼ ounces Beefeater gin
¾ ounce Noilly Prat dry vermouth
1 dash orange bitters
Lemon twist

Prepare as above.

2 ounces Bombay gin (regular, not Sapphire)
1 ounce Dolin dry vermouth
1 dash orange bitters
Lemon twist

Prepare as above.

Appendix 1: Martini Accoutrements

Bergamot-Pomelo Tincture

6 bergamots
1 (750-ml) bottle high-proof spirit (preferably Everclear)
2 pomelos

Peel the bergamots and pomelos, saving the peels. Crush the peels a bit and place them into a 1-quart jar. Fill the jar with a high-proof spirit and leave to infuse for up to 1 week. Strain the liquid from the peels and keep covered, in the refrigerator, up to 3 months.

Charred Onion–Infused Dry Vermouth

2 onions, chopped
1 (750-ml) bottle dry vermouth (preferably Noilly Prat)

If you have an open-flame grill, grill the onions until translucent. Alternatively, preheat the oven to 350°F, spread out the onions on a baking sheet, and bake until translucent. Raise the heat to 500°F and cook until the edges of the onions begin to blacken (it is okay if some pieces char completely). Remove from the grill or oven and let cool completely. Put the onions into a 1-quart jar with a lid, and add the dry vermouth. Let the vermouth infuse for 24 hours. Strain through a chinois, transfer to a clean bottle, and refrigerate. The infused vermouth will keep, covered, for up to 2 weeks.

House-Brined Olives
Makes 1 quart

907 grams Cerignola olives

16 ounces olive brine
(reserved from the Cerignola olive jars)

16 ounces Dolin blanc vermouth

16 ounces Dolin dry vermouth

22 grams juniper berries

11 grams cassia bark

7 grams fresh rosemary

14 grams lemon peel

14 grams orange peel

8 grams grapefruit peel

Combine the ingredients in a jar and seal with a lid. Let sit for at least 24 hours at room temperature before using. Once opened, store in the refrigerator for up to two weeks.

Toasted Fennel Tincture
Makes 8 ounces

⅛ cup fennel seeds

8 ounces high-proof vodka

Warm a small saucepan or skillet over medium-low heat. Toast the fennel seeds until fragrant. Let cool and combine them with the vodka in an airtight container for 7 days. Strain into a clean bottle and store at room temperature for up to 6 months.

Appendix 2: Martini Quotes

Most books about the Martini become compendiums of witty quotes about the drink—often the same witty quotes, repeated again and again, book after book. I've tried to keep such quotes to a minimum in this text, so as not to overly tread on old ground. Still, everyone loves a good Martini quip. And many of them remain quite droll, even after a thousand tellings. So, I've piled them all into this appendix— some familiar, some not, some old, some fresh—in case you'd like to trot out one or two at your next Martini party. (*Please* say you do have a Martini party in your near future.)

"I never go jogging, it makes me spill my Martini."
—George Burns

"Martinis are for adults contemplating power, sexual possibilities, or death."
—Barnaby Conrad III

"[The] supreme American gift to world culture."
—Bernard DeVoto

"When I have one Martini, I feel bigger, wiser, taller. When I have a second, I feel superlative. When I have more, there's no holding me."
—William Faulkner

"America's lethal weapon."
—Nikita Khrushchev

"Do not allow children to mix Dry Martinis. It is unseemly and they use too much vermouth."
—Steve Allen

"Martinis are the only American invention as perfect as a sonnet."
—H. L. Mencken

"He knows just how I like my Martini—full of alcohol."
—Homer Simpson

"Well, all right, but it is cold on the stomach."
—Joseph Stalin, upon first trying a Martini

"One Martini is all right. Two are too many, and three are not enough."
—James Thurber

"[A Martini] should be like sipping on a cool cloud."
—Leon Uris

"A woman with six Martinis can ruin a city."
—Clifford Odets

"[The Martini] exists to decapitate the day and fertilize the evening with its blood."
—David Wondrich

"The Martini menaces our civilization as much as the atom bomb. It may be slower, but eventual destruction will be just as absolute."
—anonymous Minneapolis bartender, 1968

Acknowledgments

I was walking down Fourteenth Street, in Manhattan, during an unseasonably warm afternoon on February 2, 2017, when, on a whim, I emailed Emily Timberlake, my editor at Ten Speed Press. "I wonder if it's time for a new Martini book?" I wrote. She responded one hour and forty minutes later: "Let's do it!"

It's the quickest book pitch turnaround I've ever experienced. For this I thank her, and her boss, publisher Aaron Wehner, deeply. I also humbly thank Julie Bennett and Ashley Pierce, who took over as editors when the beloved and much-missed Emily left the Ten Speed fold; as well as the rest of the Ten Speed team; and Lizzie Munro, who furnished all the beautiful photos herein.

I would also like to thank my agent, David Black, who always has my back, and ever lends a sympathetic ear, and all the helpful folks over at the Black Agency.

Additional thanks to Amber Appelbaum, Talia Baiocchi, Douglas Biederbeck, Greg Boehm, Dàmaris Castellanos, Toby Cecchini and St. John Frizell (for their exquisite cocktail styling), Brother Cleve, Sarah Coffin, Barnaby Conrad III, Federico Cuco, Dale DeGroff, Kevin Denton, Martin "The Librarian" Doudoroff, Lowell Edmunds, William Elliott, Simon Ford, Chloe Frechette, Kenta Goto, Philip Greene, Allison Hamlin, Bobby Heugel, John Kass, Allen Katz, Jim Kearns, Marty Marcuccilli, Ryan Maybee, Francois Monti, Will Nazar, Nicolas Palazzi, Troy Patterson, Del Pedro, Agostino Perrone, Adam Platt, Bianca Prum, Leonid Rath, Rodolfo Reich, Andy Rieger, Audrey Saunders, Adam Schuman, Anna Scudellari, Thomas Waugh, Christine Wiseman, David Wondrich, and Naren Young. I also thank the staffs at the "destination" Martini bars and restaurants: Bix, Connaught Bar, Dry Martini, Dukes Bar, the Bar at the Grill, Harry's Bar in Venice, Maison Premiere, Musso & Frank Grill, Pegu Club, and Tongue-Cut Sparrow.

Thanks, also, to my father, Robert Odin Simonson Sr., for his Martini memories, and for the love and support he has shown me over the years. Finally, my love and thanks to the two most important people in my world, my son, Asher, and my love and soulmate, Mary Kate Murray.

Index

A

Alaska, 97
Albee, Edward, 29
Allen, Steve, 159
Allies Cocktail, 120
Arno, Peter, 32
Auden, W. H., 28–29

B

Bacharach, Bert, 43
Bar Goto, 142
Barnaby Conrad III's
    Martini, 153
barspoons, 70
Beebe, Lucius, 48, 49
Beefsteak Martini, 132
Benchley, Peter, 33
Benchley, Robert, 30, 32–33
Benders, Jeff, 59
Benjamin's White Martini, 125
Bergamot-Pomelo
    Tincture, 157
Bergengren, Erik, 125
Bernard DeVoto's Martini, 150
Biederbeck, Doug "Bix,"
    88, 89
bitters, 73
Bix's Martini, 88–89
Boadas, Miguel, 49
B.O.M. (Black Olive Martini),
    64, 124
Bond, James, 45–46, 48, 112
Boothby, Bill, 17
Brackett, Charles, 30, 33
Broken Shaker, 149
Bronner, Stanley, 61
Buchwald, Art, 40
Buñuel, Luis, 30–31
Burns, George, 159
Burrough, James, 148
Butterworth, Charles, 33

C

Caen, Herb, 53
Cajun Martini, 57
Calabrese, Salvatore, 102

Carbonell, Pedro, 84
Carroll, Harrison, 33
Carter, Jimmy, 56
Cecchini, Toby, 131
Cerf, Bennett, 34
Charred Onion–Infused Dry
    Vermouth, 158
Chartreuse
    Alaska, 97
    Puritan Cocktail, 110
Cheever, John, 29
cherries, 17–18
Cipriani, Giuseppe, 122
Clariot, 127
Claude, Georges, 54
Cleve, Brother, 64–65
Club Lucky, 62, 63
cocktail strainers, 70
Coffin, Sarah, 52
Colony Restaurant, 48
Connaught Bar, 102, 108
Connaught Martini, 109
Conrad, Barnaby, III, 34, 88,
    89, 153, 159
Coward, Noël, 28
Cuco, Federico, 127
Curtis, Wayne, 34

D

Dale DeGroff's Martini, 138
Dante, 49, 67, 139
Dante House Martini, 139
Davis, Bette, 30
Day, Doris, 30
DeGroff, Dale, 20–21, 138
Déjà Vu Martini Lounge, 58
Delaplane, Stanton, 102
Desmond, Paul, 31
DeVoto, Bernard, 38, 61, 150,
    154, 159
Dirty Martini, 59, 61, 113
Drake, 64
Dry Martini, 38–41, 84–85
Dukes Bar, 102, 108
Dukes Martini, 103
Dundy, Elaine, 29

E

Early Dry Martini, 81
Edmunds, Lowell, 6, 34,
    51, 152
Elliott, William, 66, 134, 145
Embury, David, 40, 154
Ensslin, Hugo R., 120
Ewell, Tom, 30

F

FAF Martini, 148
Faulkner, William, 159
Fay, Tom, 16
Fennel Tincture, Toasted, 158
Fisher, M. F. K., 29
Fitty-Fitty, 66, 140–41
Fitzgerald, F. Scott, 27
Fleming, Ian, 46, 112
Flora Bar, 100
Ford, Gerald, 56
Four Seasons, 116
Franklin, Ami, 63

G

Gable, Clark, 30
Gallaghers Steakhouse
    Martini, 137
garnishes, 17–18, 62–65,
    73–74, 105, 133, 157
Gibson, 105
gin, 154, 155. See also
    individual martini recipes
glassware, 51–53, 70,
    88–89, 122
Goto, Kenta, 142
The Grill, 66, 67, 116
The Grill House Martini, 117

H

Haerdtl, Oswald, 52
Haimo, Oscar, 20
Hall, Frank de Peyster, 14
Hamilton, Ross, 35
Hammett, Dashiell, 29
Harry's Bar, 27, 99, 122
Harry's Bar Martini, 123

Hemingway, Ernest, 27,
99, 122
Heugel, Bobby, 146
Hevrdejs, Judy, 63
Hibrows, 64
Higgins, Jim, 62, 63
Holmes, Mike, 43
House-Brined Olives, 157

I
ice, 73
Ikeda, Shin, 65

J
jiggers, 70
Johnson, Harry, 10, 16, 82, 98
Johnson, Philip, 116

K
Kappeler, George J., 16
Kass, John, 63
Kearns, Jim, 148
Khrushchev, Nikita, 159
Kilgallen, Dorothy, 45
Kingston Trio, 31
Knickerbocker Hotel, 22, 134

L
La Floridita, 49
Lehr, Dick, 59
Lehr, Phil, 124
Lehrer, Tom, 40
Leighton, Fred, 52
Lemmon, Jack, 30
lemons, 73–74
Lewis, "Jalapeño Sam," 64
Lillet blanc
Vesper, 112
Lippold, Richard, 116
Lloyd, Alice, 13
Loesser, Frank, 31
London, Jack, 26–27
Long Island Bar, 131, 132
Lorinca, Erik, 108
Lowell Edmunds's
Martini, 152
Luli Moscato Chinato
Sauvage House
Martini, 145
Lurie, George A., 17
Luscomb, Charles, 7

M
MacLane, Mary, 13
Maison Premiere, 66, 67,
134, 145
Manhattan, 10–11, 15, 18, 53
Manhattan Club, 15, 21
Mankiewicz, Joseph, 30
Manolito, 49
maraschino liqueur
Martinez, 78
Sakura Martini, 142
Turf Cocktail, 92
Tuxedo No. 2, 100
Marcuccilli, Marty, 63
Marguerite, 98
Martin, Henry, 32
Martine, Judge, 21
Martinez, 10, 22–23, 78
Martini (general)
as clubman's drink, 14–15
color of, 11, 13–14
dirty, 59, 61, 113
dry, 38–41, 84–85
50-50s, 65–66, 140–41
first appearance of, 10
flavor of, 2
garnishes for, 17–18,
62–65, 73–74, 105,
133, 157
glassware and equipment
for, 37, 51–53, 70, 72
at home, 37–38
ingredients for, 16–18,
73–74
name of, 23–24, 26
in neon signs, 53–54, 56
-on-the-rocks, 43–44, 106
origins of, 10, 20–23
in popular culture, 26–35
popularity of, 6–7, 10–11,
15–16, 56–59, 67
quotes about, 159–60
stirring and shaking, 46,
48–49, 74
sweet, 18, 20, 86
thrown, 49
variety of opinions about,
5–6, 154–55
Martini (recipes)
Barnaby Conrad III's
Martini, 153
Beefsteak Martini, 132
Benjamin's White
Martini, 125
Bernard DeVoto's
Martini, 150
Bix's Martini, 89
B.O.M. (Black Olive
Martini), 124
Connaught Martini, 109
Dale DeGroff's
Martini, 138
Dante House Martini, 139
Dirty Martini, 113
Dry Martini, 84–85
Dukes Martini, 103
Early Dry Martini, 81
Fitty-Fitty, 141
Gallaghers Steakhouse
Martini, 137
Grill House Martini, 117
Harry's Bar Martini, 123
Lowell Edmunds's
Martini, 152
Martini (Harry
Johnson), 82
Martini (Theodore
Proulx), 83
Martini-on-the-Rocks, 106
Medium Martini, 87
Montgomery Martini, 99
Musso Martini, 95
My Martini, 156
Old King Cole
Martini, 135
Sakura Martini, 142
Sauvage House
Martini, 145
Sweet Martini, 86
Toby Cecchini's
Martini, 131
Tongue-Cut Sparrow
Martini, 147
Trash-tini, 149
Vodka Martini, 115
Martini & Rossi, 21, 23–24, 26
McDuffie, Ann, 57
McElhone, Harry, 86, 87
Medium Martini, 87
Mencken, H. L., 160
Meyer, Danny, 155
Mies van der Rohe, 116
Milk & Honey, 65, 140
mixing glasses, 70
Monroe, Marilyn, 30

Montgomery, Bernard, 99
Montgomery Martini, 99
Monti, François, 13
Morgan, Jefferson, 56
Müller, Franz Josef, 24
Musso & Frank Grill, 94
Musso Martini, 95
My Martini, 156

N
Nadine's, 58
Nash, Ogden, 13, 32, 34–35
neon signs, 53–54, 56
Newman, Frank, 24, 39, 81

O
Odets, Clifford, 160
Oldenburg, Claes, 54
Old King Cole Martini, 135
Oliver, Dorothy, 64
olives, 17–18, 74, 113
    black, 64, 124
    House-Brined Olives, 157
    stuffed, 62–65
onions, 17, 105
    Charred Onion–Infused
        Dry Vermouth, 158

P
Parker, Dorothy, 32, 33–34
Patterson, Troy, 34
Pedro, Del, 65
Pegu Club, 65–66, 140
Perrone, Agostino, 108
Petraske, Sasha, 65, 140
Phil Lehr's Steakery, 124
The Pierre, 20
Platt, Adam, 43
Policastro, Santiago
    "Pichin," 127
Pomelo Tincture,
    Bergamot-, 157
Proulx, Theodore, 10, 16, 83
Prudhomme, Paul, 57
Puritan Cocktail, 110

R
Rainbow Room, 138
Regan, Gary, 59
Reisetbauer, Hans, 155
Reynolds, Malvina, 40
Richelieu, Julio, 22
Rittenhouse Club, 16

Rockefeller, John D., 22
Roosevelt, Franklin Delano,
    26, 61
Rossi di Montelera,
    Ernesto, 21
Rudin, Max, 37
Rueda, Ruben, 94

S
Saarinen, Eero, 116
sake
    Sakura Martini, 142
    Toby Cecchini's
        Martini, 131
Saloon, 62
Saunders, Audrey, 65–66, 140
Sauvage, 67, 145
Sauvage House Martini, 145
Saxon & Parole, 61
Scannell, Eustace, 40–41
Schmidt, Marvin M., 37–38
Sinatra, Frank, 30
Slowly Shirley, 148
Smith, Donald G., 57
Smith, Jack, 33
Smith, Red, 43
Stalin, Joseph, 160
St. Charles Hotel, 21
Steele, G. F., 61
Stevens, Mick, 32
Straub, Jacques, 97
Stuart, Thomas, 98
Sullivan, Jere, 48, 49
Sweet Martini, 18, 20, 86

T
Tabla, 155
Thomas, Jerry, 10, 23, 78
Thomas, John, 13, 28
Thurber, James, 160
Toasted Fennel Tincture, 158
Toby Cecchini's Martini, 131
Tongue-Cut Sparrow Martini,
    146–47
Tooker Alley, 110
Tower, Jeremiah, 88
Townsend, Jack, 39
Trash-tini, 149
Trummer, Albert, 65
Turf Cocktail, 16, 92
Tuxedo No. 2, 100
Twain, Mark, 20

U
Uris, Leon, 160

V
Van Hecke, Tommy, 35
Venegas, Dominic, 137
Vermeire, Robert, 48
vermouth
    Charred Onion–Infused
        Dry Vermouth, 158
    choosing, 154
    color of, 11, 13–14
    in dry Martini, 38–41
    in sweet Martini, 20
    *See also individual martini
        recipes*
Vesper, 112
vodka
    B.O.M. (Black Olive
        Martini), 124
    Connaught Martini, 109
    Dirty Martini, 113
    Dukes Martini, 103
    Martini-on-the-Rocks, 106
    Trash-tini, 149
    Vesper, 112
    Vodka Martini, 44–46, 115

W
Ward, Phil, 132
Washburne, George R., 61
Waugh, Thomas, 66, 116
West, Mae, 33
White, E. B., 29
Wilder, Billy, 30, 33
Wilson, Earl, 64
Winchell, Walter, 45
Wiseman, Christine, 149
Wolfe, Tom, 54
Wondrich, David, 65, 160
Woollcott, Alexander, 32
Woolley, Monty, 39

Y
Young, Naren, 61, 139

About the Author

ROBERT SIMONSON writes about cocktails, spirits, bars, and bartenders for the *New York Times*. He is also contributing editor and columnist at PUNCH. His books include *The Old-Fashioned*, *A Proper Drink*, and *3-Ingredient Cocktails*, which was nominated for a 2018 James Beard Award. He was also a primary contributor to *The Essential New York Times Book of Cocktails*. His work, which has also appeared in *Saveur*, *Bon Appetit*, *Food & Wine*, *New York* magazine, and *Lucky Peach*, has been nominated for a total of ten Spirited Awards and two IACP Awards. A native of Wisconsin, he lives in Brooklyn.

Published in the United States by Ten Speed Press, an imprint of Random House,
a division of Penguin Random House LLC, New York.
www.crownpublishing.com
www.tenspeed.com

Ten Speed Press and the Ten Speed Press colophon are registered trademarks of
Penguin Random House LLC.

Library of Congress Cataloging-in-Publication Data.
Names: Simonson, Robert, author.
Title: The martini cocktail : a meditation on the world's greatest drink, with recipes /
    Robert Simonson.
Description: First edition. | California : Ten Speed Press, [2019] | Includes
    bibliographical references and index.
Identifiers: LCCN 2018060706 (print) | LCCN 2019000603 (ebook) |
    ISBN 9780399581229 (eBook) | ISBN 9780399581212 (hardcover : alk. paper)
Subjects: LCSH: Martinis. | Martinis–History. | LCGFT: Cookbooks.
Classification: LCC TX951 (ebook) | LCC TX951 .S58363 2019 (print) | DDC
    641.87/4–dc23
LC record available at https://lccn.loc.gov/2018060706

Hardcover ISBN: 978-0-399-58121-2
eBook ISBN: 978-0-399-58122-9

Printed in China

Design by Annie Marino

10 9 8 7 6 5 4 3 2 1

First Edition